the sixth sense

of children

the sixth sense

of children

Nurturing Your Child's Intuitive Abilities

Litany Burns

NEW AMERICAN LIBRARY

New American Library
Published by New American Library, a division of
Penguin Putnam Inc., 375 Hudson Street, New York, New York 10014, U.S.A.
Penguin Books Ltd, 80 Strand, London WC2R 0RL, England
Penguin Books Australia Ltd, Ringwood, Victoria, Australia
Penguin Books Canada Ltd, 10 Alcorn Avenue, Toronto, Ontario, Canada M4V 3B2
Penguin Books (N.Z.) Ltd, 182–190 Wairau Road, Auckland 10, New Zealand

Penguin Books Ltd, Registered Offices: Harmondsworth, Middlesex, England

First published by New American Library, a division of Penguin Putnam Inc.

First Printing, February 2002
10 9 8 7 6 5 4 3 2 1

REGISTERED TRADEMARK—MARCA REGISTRADA

LIBRARY OF CONGRESS CATALOGING-IN-PUBLICATION DATA:

Burns, Litany.
The sixth sense of children : nurturing your child's intuitive abilities / Litany Burns.
p. cm.
ISBN 0-451-20525-1 (alk. paper)
1. Children—Psychic ability. 2. Children—Psychic ability—Case studies. I. Title.

BF1045.C45 B87 2002
133.8'083—dc21
2001045252

Set in Simoncini Garamond
Designed by Leonard Telesca
Printed in the United States of America

*For all children
who live in silence
waiting to be heard*

According to the United Nations,
the six billionth human now living
on this planet was born on July 19, 1999, in California.
Every day four hundred thousand children
bring their spiritual purpose
into the human family.

Contents

Introduction

I was a child born with a "sixth sense." When I spontaneously predicted a future event I was surprised that it came to pass. I knew what people were going to say before they spoke, and I thought it was fun. I knew what animals were feeling and when people cared or didn't care for each other or me. I knew the moods of my teachers. I felt good about these feelings when they happened, and then I forgot about them. Once, when my brother was missing, I told my mother not to worry about him because I knew intuitively that he would call in a few minutes from a friend's house. I was punished when my prediction came true. My father laughed when I told him, "The dog is scared and needs to stay in my room." He ushered the dog outside, where he howled all night. I either frightened adults with my uncanny abilities or was ignored because of them.

I was not an odd child. I did the same things as other children. I excelled in school, made friends, and participated in activities. I competed in sports, I studied music, I wrote poetry. As I was growing up, no person in my family, neighborhood, school, or community recognized my intuitive talents. Those talents simply existed. Like my athletic, musical, and poetic talents, they were a part of me waiting to be discovered, developed, and used. But nothing was done about them. Whenever I voiced these sixth sense impressions I was told that I should mind my own business, that "children should be seen and not heard," that I had done something ridiculous and wrong.

I gradually stopped telling people what I "felt." I stopped listening to my natural impressions that had no logical explanation. I didn't want to be laughed at, punished, or ignored anymore. I began listening to other people's voices, feeling I could no longer know things for myself. When I followed their direction and advice I was accepted and rewarded. I could be loved. It took me twenty painful years to find my own voice again.

During all that time my sixth sense did not vanish. No matter how hard I tried to avoid my impressions, or to separate this part of myself from my life, I still felt them. I just did nothing about them. I had no idea anyone else had these experiences. Outwardly I acted just like everyone else. Inwardly I thought something must be very wrong with me. I lived intimately with members of my family and not one of us had any idea that we all experienced intuitive occurrences. There was never any discussion about my father, as a young boy, waking from a dream and calling out the name of his favorite uncle at the exact time his uncle died in an accidental fire three hundred miles away. We paid no attention to my brother's daily childhood conversations with his imaginary playmate, "Notesy." We were not aware of my mother's recurring dreams about deceased relatives. No reasons were given when my sister began seeing colors form around other people. She was taken to the eye doctor and her experience was dismissed. She did not have it again.

My family was not odd or eccentric. We had no witches or

seers among our ancestors. In fact, we did not believe in anything of the sort. We simply did not know what to say to anyone about these experiences. We did not discuss them. We thought no one else had them.

On a family excursion to a toy store at the age of twelve, I discovered what I thought to be a game. Drawn to this particular game and rejecting all others, I took it home. I thought it a strange game, since it had only two pieces. When I started playing with my Ouija board I immediately began communicating with a spirit. I had not met a spirit before, so I did not know I should be frightened. This particular spirit was very friendly. The predictions made and the information revealed by the spirit surprised and excited me. Other family members played with my toy but soon lost interest.

In the solitude of my room I continued to communicate with my new "friend." Oddly enough, I did not connect this experience with any of my earlier intuitive experiences. They were forgotten. But I told no one, not even my closest friends, about my Ouija board spirit friend. I did not want to be laughed at or told that what I was doing was silly or wrong. Thirty years later I learned that Ouija boards were spiritual tools and not games. Used knowledgeably they open up doors to places unseen.

Throughout my adolescence and college years I began to feel more comfortable with the intuitive part of myself but still not comfortable enough to discuss it with anyone else. Dreams became more vivid. Predictions came to pass. My interest in my spirit friend did not waver, but I still listened to everyone else because I believed they knew what was best for me.

The pain of living without trusting my own voice made me feel insecure and led me to seek knowledge through introspection, reading, and searching for answers to my everyday problems. I never thought to try to use my sixth sense for anything. Time and again my intuitive voice was the first to be heard and the last to be trusted. I ignored it when I needed it most, and yet it did not disappear.

After years of emotional turmoil I started to pay attention to my psychic perceptions because I began to notice that those perceptions were right. Unconscious information from dreams and waking moments was more accurate than most of the advice given to me by others. I began verbalizing this information, giving accurate insights to friends. I started writing stories, trusting my moments of inspiration. I read more about psychic phenomena, met professionals, and learned names for various intuitive abilities I had been using quite naturally since birth.

These talents became a more conscious part of my everyday life. I wanted to use them, becoming more excited as I found out how helpful they were. My self-esteem and confidence grew with each accurate insight. I did not doubt myself as much and I wanted to try more things. My life became less of a struggle within me.

Excited about these perceptions, I told friends about them spontaneously. Friends told other friends and soon I was giving psychic readings without even preparing for them. I stopped wondering how it could be possible to know such things and began using this viable part of me. Today, complete strangers sit before me and as a professional I trust the knowledge given about them and their personal lives.

As soon as I began to learn how important my sixth sense was for clarity and confidence in my life I started teaching other people what I knew. My first class was with children, since I remembered what childhood had been like for me. The children, ages seven to fourteen, were excited. Without hesitation they enjoyed the exercises, happy to feel good about abilities that came so easily to them. Watching their excitement and easy acceptance of their natural, innate talents, I thought about all the silent years of my childhood.

This sixth sense in children is not isolated or unique, as most thriller movies or books would have you believe. There are millions of very normal intuitive children playing, working, sleeping, and dreaming all over the world today. They play in city streets, on the fields of farmlands, or in suburban backyards. They are poor and rich; black, white, yellow, and brown; short and tall; male and female. Physical background does not limit their special abilities. Each child's sixth sense is as natural as laughing, loving, learning, and breathing.

Yet there are many intuitive children today who are silent. They do not talk about their imaginary friends. They are unable to focus or achieve their potential in classrooms. They are highly emotional and sensitive to their environment. They have low self-esteem. They hold back what they see or feel for fear of sounding strange or stupid or odd. They are bright, active, artistic, athletic, and loving, and yet they suffer alone inside themselves. They do not know why they feel things so deeply, why they see things that may not be visible to others, how they can tell when things are going to happen, why they react so strongly to what other people say or do. Some become depressed, hyperactive, stressed out, or enraged, or even violent.

In a technological world obsessed with virtual reality, cyberspace conversations, techno music, and a future potentially filled with food shortages, air pollution, global warming, health hazards, and unknown living conditions, children will need to be physically and spiritually able. Now, more than ever, children need to remain in touch with their inner voice, their internal strength, creative ideas, self-love, and intuition in order to have more wholly satisfied lives.

The Sixth Sense of Children invites you into that inner world. It offers insights that can be applied in a very modern world. It does not exclude any religious or spiritual beliefs or knowledge any reader may already hold. Open to everyone, it offers a dynamically fresh way of looking at the true potential in each of us. Acknowledging these innate talents and learning to use them tangibly in everyday life can help children, parents, friends, teachers, siblings, and relatives realize their true potential at home, in school, and in life.

The Sixth Sense of Children unlocks the silence so that children can openly develop talents they already possess to deepen their understanding of themselves, their peers and social environment, and the rapidly changing world around them. To that end, many of the exercises and techniques included were created specifically for children and families to enjoy and share together as they develop and discover their natural intuitive abilities. The book offers a chance for families to examine a whole new way of understanding the family as a growing unit made up of unique individuals. Finally, it extends an open invitation to all adults of any age to rediscover their own sixth sense and actively enjoy the child alive and well within.

With this information I reach out to the child in all of us who surprises us with insight, touches us with loving, connects us to one another, makes us laugh, helps us cry, and keeps us caring and whole. I write with the hope of unself-consciously taking hypocrisy and misinformation out of the closet and airing it so we can be openly educated and wise. *The Sixth Sense of Children* calls out for the voice of every child to be heard—plainly, clearly, and with delight and love.

"I feel something burning, Mama," six-year-old Carla said while her family sat eating dinner. Her mother checked the stove and all the appliances. Everything was fine. "I still feel something burning," Carla insisted. Annoyed by Carla's disruption, her father rose from the table and checked all the electrical outlets, including those in the garage and the basement. Carla was told to finish her meal and get ready for bed.

That night, while everyone was asleep, Carla woke up and ran into her parents' bedroom. "Daddy! Daddy! There's a fire in the house!" Although he smelled no trace of smoke, her father sleepily went down the stairs to inspect the house. When he reached the laundry room he found the beginning of an electrical fire, which he quickly put out, ending the possibility of a disastrous blaze.

Ten-year-old Michelle and Teresa were best friends even though they lived two towns apart. Each would instantly know when the other was sick or in trouble.

One day, while Teresa was sick at home and Michelle was in school, Teresa felt her friend was in danger. Unable to reach her, and knowing that Michelle was walking home from school, Teresa sent her a message from her mind. "Don't go home the same way. Go another way." Teresa had no idea why she was doing this. She just knew she had to keep repeating the message in her mind. "Don't go home the same way. Go another way." Without thinking, Michelle suddenly turned away from a group of children who were about to cross the street and headed down another street toward home. Shortly afterward, a car careened out of control and

*The stories at the beginning of each chapter are based upon years of experience working with intuitive children.

struck some of the children who had been walking with Michelle, injuring them.

Seven-year-old Pedro could see angels. He only saw them when they had something to say to him. One Saturday an angel told Pedro a secret message to give his father. "Daddy," Pedro began, trying to get his father's attention while he was working at his computer. "Pedro, please," his father said. "I'm busy now. I'll talk to you later." Pedro's angel kept telling Pedro to give his father the message. Patiently Pedro waited. Finally Pedro said to his father before leaving the room, "Daddy, you have to pick the blue one. Pick the blue one."

Unbeknownst to Pedro, his father was working on a complicated problem on-line with his office, using two color codes. Each code represented a set of variables that held separate solutions to a telecommunications formula he and several researchers were exploring for his company—a formula that could earn a lot of money. Throwing up his hands in frustration, Pedro's father laughingly accessed the blue program in his computer and studied it. Within an hour he and his colleagues discovered the solution they had been seeking for two months.

1

What Is the Sixth Sense of Children?

Mother: "Look at the baby! He's trying to tell us something."
Father: "He's moving his hands. He wants something."
Mother: "He wants the little fluffy elephant."
Father: "He doesn't want that. He wants to be held."
The father lifts the baby. The baby cries. He hands the baby
  to the mother. The baby continues crying.
Father: "Give him the teddy bear right next to him."
The baby continues crying.
Mother: "Here." She places the fluffy elephant beside the
  baby. The baby ceases to cry.

Coincidence? Chance? Mother's intuition?

  Or another level of communication?

  All children are naturally intuitive. From the moment they
first enter the physical world as infants they spontaneously rely
on their sixth sense for communication and protection. It is
what they innately know. Like animals, they rely on these

primary unspoken impressions for their physical daily survival before language, mental, and social skills have developed.

Besides using their physical tactile senses of taste, touch, seeing, hearing, and smelling, babies relate to people and their environment using this other set of talents commonly referred to as their sixth sense, intuition, or psychic abilities.

Place an infant in a room with many people and he will unself-consciously be drawn to the person no one would expect to give him comfort—the grumpy old uncle, the timid adolescent, the uninterested neighbor, the preoccupied aunt. Every family has such stories, told about the baby snuggling in the lap of the relative none of the others can stand, the cat rubbing lovingly against the legs of the one person in the room who "hates cats." Why does this happen? Without the intrusion of mental thoughts or defenses the infant or animal intuitively "senses" the deeper loving of the person and trusts it, while adults may not.

Kaitlin was eight months old. Distant relatives of the Sturber family were visiting. They were gathered around the kitchen table sharing coffee and cake while Kaitlin slept in her mother's arms. Only one relative was absent. Uncle Theo, not one for socializing, had moved to the living room to watch a baseball game on television. Soon the other men joined him, including Kaitlin's father, whom Kaitlin adored.

Upon awakening, Kaitlin struggled to the floor and began to crawl toward the living room, disregarding the outstretched arms of her loving relatives. She deliberately crawled past her father and toward Uncle Theo, who ignored her. She grabbed Uncle Theo's pant leg and with great persistence pulled herself upright. She began to cry. Without taking his eyes off the screen, Uncle Theo dutifully lifted the child into his lap and did nothing more. Happily, Kaitlin fell asleep in her uncle's lap.

Parapsychological studies have shown other interesting aspects concerning intuitive behavior in babies. It has been reported that when an infant is placed in the same room as a person who feels tired or stressed, without that person showing any outward signs of his condition, the infant will react by being jumpy, fretful, or agitated for no apparent reason.

Tests have even shown that when a child is placed in a room or house where an argument or emotional situation took place at an earlier time, the child will respond to the "vibes" or energy left behind, even when none of the people involved are present. Often an infant becomes upset when a mother or caretaker, without giving any outward signal, plans to leave for a few hours later in the day. The child may cling to her without explanation or demand more of her attention and time.

Timothy was a happy baby. Nothing seemed to bother him. Then his mother noticed that every time she began mentally planning to go shopping with a neighbor, he would begin to cry and become agitated. She experimented to see if these instances were related. She made her plans only when Timothy was sleeping. Without her acting any differently toward him, he consistently would react on the day she was leaving, regardless of the time or date. Chalking it up to coincidence or her unconscious behavior toward him, she was surprised when a friend unexpectedly called to invite her to lunch and Timothy began to exhibit the same agitation moments after she got off the telephone.

Babies rely on their sixth sense—their intuitive or psychic abilities—to communicate with us long before they learn to speak. This psychic talent, the ability to send and receive mental impressions from one living being to another, is called telepathy. It is the most common of all our psychic abilities, and it is commonly used by babies before they comprehend words or language. In fact, infants often encourage adults to rediscover their own telepathic skills when communicating with them.

This ability in adults, often called "mother's intuition," is widespread throughout every culture in history between mothers or parents and their offspring. Prior to birth and while children are physically developing, mothers intuitively know their children's needs and desires, and communicate freely with them. After birth, more often than not, the baby is telepathically communicating with his mother because he needs changing, protection, loving, or emotional reinforcement.

Children, long before they can actually speak, use their natural intuitive abilities to sense adults' emotional needs. Often a small child, for no apparent reason, will suddenly stop what he is doing and rush over to an adult and give him an extra kiss or hug. As if guided by some nonverbal cue, the child may present an adult with a cherished toy and then calmly return to his play without mentally knowing that the adult was experiencing stress or disappointment at that moment. Children also sense the vibrations, or energy, of physical places.

Garry, a usually tranquil child, began crying the moment his parents settled into an old inn while on vacation. Although his surroundings were quiet, Garry refused to sleep all night. When they moved to another old inn at another location in the same town, Garry slept peacefully. His parents later learned from people in the town that a murder had been committed in the first inn several years earlier.

As children develop physically they learn to verbalize. They often combine their newly learned verbal skills with their reliable nonverbal telepathic communication, thereby creating a great understanding gap between themselves and adults. Their lack of words can often be confusing. They become frustrated when adults do not understand what they are trying to say.

A child may say, for example, "Johnny come." But that may mean he wants you to come to him. His mixture of learned language and intuitive language may be in sync with him but not for the adult who relies totally on verbal language for communication.

As children begin to rely more heavily on their verbal skills for communication, they still retain their telepathic skills. When under emotional pressure or in tension-producing situations, they may revert to telepathic communication, because that is where they feel safest expressing their primary needs. Adults may see this as reverting back to baby ways or being immature. But children are simply relying on what they know to be real and helpful to them.

Interestingly, adults often do the same thing unconsciously. Especially in times of emotional stress or confrontation, adults may expect the others involved to know and understand the intention of their words or actions or deepest thoughts without verbally expressing them fully. They revert to the primary telepathic talents they used as infants when they feel most deeply threatened. Think about it. Have you done this?

Often, within the family, older siblings, having "outgrown" their needs for using their telepathic talents, will naturally revert back to them to translate to adults the needs or desires of younger siblings.

When two-year-old Keisha began to cry in frustration after pointing to her new shoes and saying, "Foot. Foot," her mother thought she was in pain. She removed Keisha's shoe, examined her foot, and found nothing wrong. She replaced the shoe, only to have Keisha wail more loudly. Afraid of hurting her child, the mother put the shoe down. Keisha wailed more. Finally Keisha's seven-year-old brother, Kevin, entered the room.

"What do you want?" Kevin asked the child. Keisha looked up at him with pleading eyes and continued to cry. Without saying a word Kevin went to Keisha's closet, took out another pair of shoes, and started putting them on her feet. Instantly Keisha stopped crying.

Like foreign-language interpreters, older siblings become translators of nonverbal communication between younger siblings and the adult world. Understanding the younger child on an intuitive level, the brother or sister can sense the deep needs and feelings that the child cannot yet verbalize. Many adults will automatically ask an older sibling to explain to them what a child wants or needs.

Joshua was seven years old and his autistic brother Jake was four. Jake was unable to communicate verbally, but Joshua always knew what Jake needed. Very calmly he would approach their mother while Jake sat on his bed, staring at the window, and tell her when Jake wanted to go to the bathroom or when Jake was hungry. Every time the mother followed Joshua's direction, Jake responded positively. Joshua was not more caring toward Jake than their mother was, he simply understood telepathically what Jake was asking.

In fact, telepathic communication is a very common form of communication among all siblings in families. Since it was their initial way of speaking to one another, it is easier and faster—a kind of code that allows them to keep the secrets between them from adults. How many times have you and your sister, brother, cousin, or friend communicated between you without words when parents or teachers tried to get information from any of you? It is a simple and safe way for children to remain in touch with each other while avoiding adults' intrusion.

Although most adults in the modern world hardly focus on using their telepathic talents, there are cultures and tribal groups that openly rely on these talents. The San Blas Indians of Panama, the Indians of Manitoba, and indigenous peoples of New Guinea and Samoa use telepathy as a natural means of everyday communication between adults and children. For them it is a natural and useful way to understand one another instantly.

Twins also rely more openly on the telepathic connections between them and use these connections throughout their adult lives. Because of these close bonds, each twin intuitively knows what the other twin is thinking, feeling, or knowing.

> *When four-year-old Kelly badly scraped her knee playing on the swing at a friend's house, across town her twin sister Deirdre, sick at home with the flu, grabbed the same knee at the same time and began crying in pain. Moments later their mother received a phone call from the friend's mother telling her about Kelly's accident.*

There have been countless documented stories of how twins use their sixth sense to find each other after being separated for years; how a twin can physically feel what the other twin is experiencing even though miles or continents may separate them; how twins have a hidden language between them that other siblings may not have. In the Zulu, Baganda, and Yoruba peoples of Africa, twins are thought to possess magical abilities to foretell the future due to their shared telepathic powers.

Children, even twins, do not "possess" a more advanced sixth sense than adults. They simply are more open, more in touch with using their natural intuitive talents in their physical lives.

In ancient cultures like legendary Atlantis, Egypt, Greece, and Rome young children who showed exceptional psychic talents were admired, often revered, by their families and society. Intuitively gifted children were selected as potential leaders with authority and spiritual knowledge that would benefit the entire society. Ancient Greeks consulted with astrologers before a child was born, wanting to know how to encourage him in both his physical and spiritual development. Egyptians welcomed the intuitive talents of their children as "godly gifts," nurturing them with great respect for their beneficent powers.

Even modern culture, focused on technology and rational thought, is filled with stories of people with positive supernatural powers and spiritual knowledge in folktales and fairy tales, contemporary literature, art, comic books, superstitions, and the Bible. The people of every culture on earth teach their young with creation stories and fables involving supernatural beings with beneficent powers. In today's television cartoons and children's books such beings appear with modern twists.

Yet, in a modern world, all too soon children are purposely taught that rational thinking must dominate their primary intuitive senses. Because of the deliberate emphasis on logical reason and intellect, children relying on their intuitive perceptions begin to question them. They doubt their use in a world that believes "mental thinking" equals "reward." The emphasis placed on physical intelligence rather than spiritual knowledge and intuition teaches Western children that mental logic produces greater accomplishment than spiritual experiences. Psychic perceptions and abilities, although depended upon from birth, are never discussed and are often viewed as weird, scary, or problematic rather than stimulating, admirable, or thought-provoking as children mature. Those children who remain overtly connected to their psychic impressions and rely on their intuition find that the outside world presents problems.

Problems and Possibilities

Often neglected, overlooked, or misunderstood by parents and teachers, this sixth sense in children creates a variety of problems for them in a world geared to logical problem solving.

Such a world disapproves when a child speaks or acts without reason, or when his dreams have no tangible meaning. It is critical when he responds or reacts to the feelings of a parent or teacher without rational explanation, or when he cannot stop talking or fidgeting. When a child does not memorize his lessons or asks too many questions or wants to look beyond a plausible explanation for things, he is told: "Pay attention," "Sit still," "Be quiet," "Don't be so touchy," "You're so stupid," "That's crazy," "Mind your own business." A sensitively intuitive child takes adults literally at their word.

Todd was a happy child. He related to people and was perceptive and bright. But in ninth grade he began to have problems. Telling no one, he sensed that his teacher and the principal were conspiring to falsify grades of certain students in his class. He had no physical proof, only a feeling to back up his theory. Distrusting of his teacher, he turned in less homework. His teacher reprimanded him, and this made him dislike her more. Soon he began cutting classes. His parents punished him. When he blurted out his thoughts, he was asked for proof and told to buckle down and do his work. His grades suffered. He began to lose faith in himself and he ceased caring about his earlier goals.

It was not until Todd reached tenth grade that the conspiracy was uncovered. It involved several young athletes, who were expected to help the school win important sectionals to raise publicity and gain money. The teacher and

*the principal, deeply implicated, were fired. Todd's victory
was bittersweet, as he continued to distrust the system and
family that did not believe him in the beginning.*

Todd's situation may have been unique, but his problems
were not. Many children are made to suffer repeatedly for the
natural and spontaneous use of their intuitive talents. Like
Todd, they begin to suppress their insights and their urge for
expression. They distrust their intuition and doubt themselves
when making decisions and choices, or when trying new things.
They develop psychological blocks that stifle other talents they
might possess, hinder their potential, and hurt their self-esteem
at an early age.

In school, at home, and with friends, intuitive children begin
to have problems. They withdraw, unable to compete in an intellectually driven world. When their instincts caution against
outwardly good relationships, the distrust that forms leads them
to limit their activities. Incapable of explaining themselves, they
may use their intuitive abilities to manipulate people so they will
leave them alone and not expect so much from them. They may
build strong defensive walls to prevent themselves from reacting
emotionally to injustices and stressful emotional situations in
their immediate environment. They may avoid competition or
go overboard to please people, disregarding their own feelings
for the sake of approval and acceptance. In the eyes of their
schools and the societies in which they live, intuitive children
may not seem exceptional at all.

It has been suggested that Thomas Edison, Albert Einstein,
Leonardo da Vinci, Winston Churchill, and Emily Dickinson
were intuitive children who suffered during childhood for their
talents.

Thomas Edison, with his uncanny creativity, had such great
trouble learning the alphabet that he was not allowed to start

school until he was eight years old. Winston Churchill, one of the great leaders of the Western world, was a precocious painter who had extreme difficulty learning and conforming to the structured atmosphere of school. Albert Einstein, one of the most respected scientists of the twentieth century, did not speak until age four and did not read until he was nine years old, yet felt an enduring spiritual and creative connection to things beyond the physical world. Leonardo da Vinci saw futuristic images in his dreams and imagined inventions like flying machines and helicopters that were thought to be ludicrous during his time. Emily Dickinson, so empathetic and sensitive, withdrew into the security of her room at a young age and wrote mature poems about universal feelings of love and life.

Children in families and schools throughout the contemporary world who might be future innovators, artists, and leaders share similar problems. Standardized Western schooling with its emphasis on memorization and fact does not incorporate the natural intuitive ways in which children learn. Children are visual. They are conceptual. Intuitively they learn through understanding. Seeing the whole picture of a problem, situation, person, or process, they then will naturally retain the sum of its parts. They innately do not conceive of the parts before the whole is known or learned.

If a small child is taught that Zimbabwe is a country in Africa, he will work hard to remember it, but it will have no meaning for him and he will soon forget it. If a child is shown a map of the world or of the continent of Africa and told where Zimbabwe is located, he will be more apt to retain the information. If, in addition, he is taught or shown the people and their culture, he will remember facts about the people of Zimbabwe who live in a country on the continent of Africa. All parts connect conceptually to him. They are not separate and meaningless to him. Once the whole is understood, he can naturally separate the parts and learn about them.

Western learning is based solely on the premise that the sum of the parts is equal to the whole. But when all the learning perceptions of children are used, the whole is learned first and the parts naturally follow. Understanding the relationship of facts to something greater and visual allows children to use all of their talents and integrate their learning in a natural way. It has been of great concern that American children perform poorly on standardized tests compared to children of other industrialized countries. Every year American children are taught to memorize their lessons for a test; once the test is over, the facts are promptly discarded. Without the deeper concepts taught, the lessons are quickly forgotten. How many Americans remember the date of Lincoln's Gettysburg Address or can recite anything more than its first line? Yet almost everyone remembers the story of Abe Lincoln's childhood, of his educating himself by candlelight in a log cabin. Methods of teaching that incorporate a holistic approach to information have more success in getting children to retain information and to find real-life applications for it.

In classrooms and at home, many intuitive children who physically responded to their environment as infants also become disruptive around others. Without knowledge they react to the energies around them.

Sammy had always been an active child, but his behavior became increasingly animated whenever he was in class. He was a sweet and bright child, but he just couldn't sit still. Left alone, he could play by himself for hours and not create a problem. In school, he was unable to stay in his seat; he would fidget at his desk and distract other students, and ask countless questions. His parents could not understand his behavior and became increasingly angry with him.

Sammy had no idea what was wrong. He could not tell his parents anything that was bothering him. He liked his teacher. He did not want the attention being given to him. He tried to sit in his seat and remain quiet but found he could do it only for a while. He became increasingly frustrated and unhappy and was finally given medication to calm him down.

Many children who are still in touch with their intuitive talents face similar problems in school. Although children tested for Attention Deficit Disorder (ADD) and other physical or mental disorders may exhibit similar behavior, there are children with no family history or physical, behavioral, or psychological problems that act out in class or become agitated or active for no logical reason. They intuitively react and actively respond to the emotional feelings and energy around them. Intuitive children may not know why they are suddenly angry or cannot remain in their seats in a crowded classroom or at the dinner table where people are quietly angry, upset, or frustrated. They are like lightning rods for the emotions of the people or energy in the room or house. Many times people around them show no outward sign of their emotions, and perhaps are not even in touch with them. Empathetic by nature, some intuitive children will react physically and unconsciously to the confusion or emotions around them. This behavior is clearly evident with two very young siblings. One sibling will start to cry and within moments the other child is also crying for no apparent reason. Animals display the same reaction. Place two cats in a room and if one cat begins to cry the other will soon cry with it.

The people around disruptive intuitive children are usually unaware of these possible causes for their behavior. And when teachers or parents become increasingly upset or frustrated by their behavior, they become even more active or agitated. Adults with no intuitive understanding of their "invisible" dilemmas add to their problems. The children are ultimately reprimanded, disciplined, punished, or ridiculed by teachers and classes or family members, and incorrectly treated for psychological or physiological problems. They are given counseling, psychiatric treatment, or drugs for a condition that needs further scrutiny.

Children who have tested negative for organic disorders or neurological disorders are probably acutely intuitive. And there are simple remedies to help intuitive children restore themselves to their natural balance:

- Give them a few minutes of extra play in a separate part of the room.
- Change their seat location in the class.
- Let them be involved in a short creative project.
- Encourage them to verbalize their momentary feelings without judgment.

Any of these simple techniques or a combination of them will allow intuitive children to return to their natural behavior without provocation. Finding a simple routine that works—whether it be letting them run outside and play a little longer than expected when they begin to feel "edgy" or finding a creative outlet that engages their interest—will go a long way to allow such children to feel good about themselves, gain focus, retain emotional stability, and show their natural intelligence.

Usually precocious, children with sixth sense talents are also innately emotionally sensitive to the feelings of others. Unable to maturely verbalize these feelings or differentiate them from their own, they have emotional difficulty during times of stress or family tensions. Such a child may deeply feel his mother's pain, his father's worry, his brother's sorrow. With no outlet for these feelings he may become moody, withdrawn, or given to sudden emotional outbursts. He may start fights, act out, or become severely depressed, isolating himself from others at home or at school. His "hypersensitivity" may lead to difficulty socializing. What is seen as social ineptitude may be a desperate battle to maintain inner balance and emotional equilibrium when the world is too much for him to handle.

Honest communication will enable him to verbalize his perceptions so that he can separate and understand his emotions. He can know his insights are right. He can learn to explore the differences in his feelings when in contact with others around him. He needs to be able to express his feelings, no matter how strange they may sound, and not feel his sensitivity is bad or wrong. Every nuance of his day does not have to be scrutinized, but when his behavior changes, gentle kindness is just as important as communication. An empathetic child responds to kindness and intuitively appreciates the effort made by someone else in his behalf. Even if there is no immediate solution that gets to the basis of his feelings, caring will remind him that he can respect what he feels and that the door is always open for future discussion.

Children who make constant use of their psychic wits for daily survival also suffer for their invisible talents.

Tyrell knew the street. He knew when to lay low and when he could hang out without being scared. He protected his sister and her friends without any outward warning when he felt things were unsafe. He knew he wasn't smart in school like the other kids, so he held back. He didn't study because he already knew the teacher was overwhelmed and he could get by. The street was where he got his education.

Such an example may be exaggerated, but many children from economically impoverished areas rely on their psychic impressions every day and night for physical survival. Inside the classroom they fall between the cracks of structured learning. The "go-to person" on the street, admired for his finely honed sensitivities and knowledge may not be able to retain information correctly in the classroom due to an incompatible system of education.

Thought to be suffering from poor language skills, he may be superior to his peers in intellectual potential but unable to express himself. Intuitively attuned to insincere gestures or dishonest actions, he may sense condescending attitudes, prejudice, and rejection in the classroom. He may not turn in homework or participate in discussion, or he may become disruptive in class to compensate for this inability even though he is bright and talented. Since he is able to read people's weaknesses and strengths, he intuitively knows how to find his way out of uncomfortable situations in the classroom while struggling to maintain his sense of pride. In this way a child of great potential falls short in a system that does not serve his total needs.

Given honest respect and genuine caring, street-smart children intuitively sense people's real intent and respond positively. With added assurance and knowledge about his process of learning, a highly sensitive, bright, and talented child from any background can become the mentally productive individual that he is.

Adults can become more aware of intuitive children's problems through simple daily observation. When does a child exhibit behavior that is not usual for him? What other circumstances or people surround him? How well do you communicate with him? How honest are you in your own actions and feelings?

Children learn by watching. They learn by doing. In an open atmosphere that encourages children to find new ways, ideas, and activities, an intuitive child can discover and gain acceptance of his talents and capabilities without feeling different. Here are some suggestions that may be helpful:

• When a child voices his impressions, regardless of how illogical or unfounded they may seem, hear him out without judging or dismissing what he has to say. If you do not understand, ask him to explain. If he has difficulty verbalizing his insights, give him time to gather his thoughts. Be patient. He will learn to respect his perceptions and find ways of voicing them. Along the way he will learn not to reject or internalize information and will improve his verbal skills. Using both his intuitive and his physical resources will help him to integrate all parts of himself.

• If a child is having trouble learning a certain subject, don't force him to conform to a specific learning method. Work with him to create innovative ways to make learning easier and more meaningful for him. If a child is having trouble memorizing his multiplication tables, use visual cues like colors or objects—a red balloon for the number one, a yellow and red balloon for the number two, and so on—to help him focus and retain information. He will feel good about the tangible (mental) and intangible (creative) parts of himself.

• Self-guidance and self-reliance are important for the development of a child's personal identity. When possible, let him try things his own way. Allow him to use his own spontaneous process whenever possible. By relying on his own inner resources he will learn to value his uniqueness. Stimulated by these discoveries, he will discover study habits that will be fruitful for him.

• Children's curiosity leads them to seek knowledge. Overt negative reactions or impatience prompts them to repress their insatiable appetite for learning. An intuitive child will respond to the moods and responses of others, either forgoing his own way of doing things to please a parent, teacher, or adult friend or holding back his potential due to disapproval and embarrassment. Be human but honest. He will sense your honesty and be more confident in his learning.

• Notice if a child is edgy or uncomfortable. Allow him time to release his physical and nonphysical energies accumulated throughout the day. Children look forward to free unrestricted time for play or talk before moving on to another learning activity. A break between periods of concentration will ensure a child the chance to balance and focus his energy so that he will feel comfortable during a lesson and will enable him to maintain a level focus so that physical distractions do not diminish his self-esteem.

• Encourage a child to feel good about his differences and similarities with others. Allow him to feel good about his own way of doing things so that he can feel proud of himself. Respecting his individuality will encourage him to learn from and respect others with an open mind.

• Let a child talk about his dreams or intuitive experiences even if they are without logical basis or seem foreign to you. Help him explore his perceptions even when you do not have all the answers. Your being open to understanding and learning about all parts of him will allow him to feel free to discuss things with you. Sharing intuitive experiences and impressions among family members allows him to participate in a shared and nonjudgmental atmosphere.

• Appreciate his sensitivity and do not treat it as his failing. Since he is very sensitive to everything around him, an intuitive child needs to find comfortable ways of expressing what he is experiencing. He needs to see his sensitivity as a positive benefit. In a supportive atmosphere, such a child will feel good about his feelings instead of inhibiting them.

• In emotionally painful situations (divorce, death of a family member, illness), let a child voice his feelings. Empathetic to those around him, he often has conflicting responses that, left unexpressed, become internalized. He needs to be reassured, held, loved, and told he is not to blame for things he did not cause, that it is fine to feel whatever he is feeling, and that he is appreciated for his deep caring and concern.

• A child needs to feel like an individual and be encouraged to find his way. An intuitively sensitive child is frequently seen as fragile or inept because of his obvious emotional vulnerabilities. With good intentions, overprotective parents may thwart his development, inhibit him, and make him doubt his inner impressions. A child's self-discovery and self-reliance can be encouraged simply by allowing him to take his own steps in his own way at his own time, in the knowledge that you are nearby, allowing him to take needed chances.

There is no rulebook for adults to follow concerning children's intuition. The best thing to do is trust your own intuition. A child will be naturally grateful for that. No one is perfect. Everyone grows and changes, including adults.

Children, intuitively attuned, easily accept people's limitations and their sincerity. They embrace people for who they are. They respect honesty. They respond to love. If you have trouble understanding an impression the child verbalizes or are confused by certain behavior, voice your feelings lovingly and honestly. An intuitive child will gratefully accept your shortcomings and try harder. He will reflect your loving, and together you may learn more than expected. The greatest help anyone can give a child is to accept him. Let him teach you about his feelings, his hunches and impressions. Let him make mistakes without ridicule so he can feel good and not be disappointed in himself. Let him learn to verbalize his deepest feelings. Then he will want to use all of his talents without excluding any aspect of himself.

Common Questions and Answers

What is the difference between a psychological problem and one resulting from an intuitive experience?

Many children face psychological problems that are not necessarily intuitive in nature. Sometimes it is difficult to separate clearly a psychological problem from the results of an intuitive perception. They can be somewhat interrelated, since both psychological and intuitive reactions are integral parts of a child. Rather than limit possibilities to just one category, adults should be open to considering all possible avenues of help and exploration, including the understanding of intuitive perceptions. Encouraging a child to verbalize his impressions and observing his behavior is the best way to define the problem and identify the proper course of treatment. Limiting possible solutions to one mode of treatment, however, may limit the usefulness of that treatment.

Is it better to work with children individually or to work with them in a group when helping them develop their sixth sense?

Both group and individual settings can be helpful to a child developing his intuitive/psychic abilities. Having others around with similar talents and perceptions can reinforce and motivate some children. They enjoy knowing that others share their talents. Other children, sensitive to the reactions or energies of many people, may find it easier to focus during individual activities. If a child shies away from group activities, let him practice individually and participate in group settings at a later time as he wishes.

How far should adults go when helping children develop their sixth sense? Should there be limits?

When exploring intuitive abilities, children find their own natural limits. Forcing a child to conform to a schedule reduces his natural spontaneity and creative impulses. He may become frustrated when forced to adhere to routines or restrictions. Let his interest lead him. If time and circumstances are factors, remind him. If he becomes overwhelmed or upset by an intuitive situation, encourage him to talk about his feelings to better understand the experience rather than allow misunderstanding or fear to deter him from further discovery.

Is there a specific atmosphere, place, or time of day that enhances a child's development of his intuitive abilities?

The best atmosphere for a child is one that is encouraging and open without being judgmental. Intuitive abilities, being natural, are experienced all the time. Structuring a time, place, or situation for a child may deprive him of his natural timing and the knowledge that his abilities are available for exploration anytime and anywhere. He needs to know that his talents are an integral part of him and do not go away. With practice, they become more apparent and helpful.

What if an intuitive experience or ability frightens a child?

There are times when new experiences, information, or insight—intuitive or not—can frighten or overwhelm a child. Impressions may seem too vivid or frightening, a prediction may come to pass, energy may be too abundant and overpowering. Encourage the child to verbalize his feelings so that his fear diminishes. Help him to understand that he does not cause things to happen. Remember that intuitive children are empathetic. If you are frightened or angered or confused by his experience, his feelings will be heightened by your emotions. Work together to explore and resolve feelings that are uncomfortable for both of you.

Will some children develop their sixth sense more than other children within the same family?

Each child's nonphysical and physical talents are unique. Two children in the same family may be talented telepathically but one may consistently use his telepathic ability as a daily part of his communication. The other may not use telepathy for years and come to develop it later in his life. Each child deserves the freedom to discover his potential at his own speed and in his own time without comparisons.

Should adults share their present or childhood intuitive experiences with children?

Part of the process of growing is sharing experiences with others. Relating personal intuitive or psychic experiences to children enables them to know they are not alone in their perceptions and talents and will strengthen the loving, enduring bond of experience between you.

At what age should you explain to a child what he is experiencing with his sixth sense?

Explaining intuitive abilities depends, like any other explanation, on a child's interest. Be creative when explaining intuitive instances to him so he can explore them with you. If he questions things that happen to, or around, him, investigate ways to find answers together: reading books, seeking out professionals, sharing common experiences. If a child is uninterested, reacts negatively, or is confused, take cues from his behavior and do not pursue the matter. He will let you know when or if he wants to know more. Keep lines of communication open so that he can feel free to discuss what he is feeling and know that you are there to support and help him with his discoveries. Your loving participation is more important than anything you can teach him about his intuitive talents.

"Don't worry Mama," three-year-old Kimberly Jean blurted out before leaving home for nursery school. "Grampa is going to be all right." Her mother did not know what she was talking about since both of Kimberly Jean's grandfathers were perfectly fine and had visited for her birthday party only a week before. Four hours later, Kimberly's mother received a phone call informing her that her father had just been in an automobile accident near his home forty miles away but was unharmed.

Four-year-old Jake was sitting at the dining room table drawing pictures. Upstairs his older sister was preparing to take some newly prescribed medicine for her asthma. Without warning Jake rushed upstairs and grabbed the bottle off the sink, refusing to give it to her. Retrieving the medicine from Jake, his mother noticed that the pills were not what had been prescribed for her daughter but had another customer's name on the label.

Thirteen-year-old Samantha and her mother met a pregnant neighbor while shopping at the grocery store. After the woman left, Samantha was visibly distressed. She told her mother she felt the neighbor's baby was going to die, but she would have another healthy baby girl the next year. Her mother said nothing to the neighbor. Three nights later the neighbor was rushed to the hospital and had a stillborn delivery. A year after that she gave birth to a healthy nine-pound girl.

2

An Old Soul in a Young Body

"Yes, that's my daughter. She's five but she's going on forty."
"I don't know where she gets it from. She seems to know more than me sometimes."
"He's just like a little old man."

Many psychic children have old souls even though their bodies are quite young. Intuitively they exhibit wisdom, creative thoughts, and insights with a maturity that goes far beyond their few years on earth.

These "old souls" may act like "little old men" or "little old women" as soon as they begin to talk. They may surprise us with their uncanny insights, mature behavior, and deep loving. Deeply wise in spiritual matters, they may be very immature in their physical ways. They may be able to explain why people should not go to war and then do something silly like untying their shoelaces and tripping themselves. Their physical behavior is not usually consistent with their innate wisdom. They are learning the ways of the body while retaining the knowledge of the soul.

The soul is timeless. A spiritual part of all creation, it is formed from the loving energy that creates us all. This positive loving, universal in encompassing all religious beliefs, is acknowledged and shared most easily by children. Recently attached to that loving source, they come to us in new bodies that still embrace that true essence. The aspects of the soul exceed material wealth and physical knowledge. Without a sense of his soul a child would feel intensely disconnected, isolated, and incomplete. His sensitivity to life would be dulled and his creativity and resourcefulness would be limited. He would feel no connection to the deeper meaning of things. Intuitively, he senses this "soul connection" in all living beings.

Once a child is born, his body is his soul's house for the duration of his physical life. His body allows him to share language, ideas, thoughts, and emotions, and to interact with other souls housed in bodies.

A soul that has so much knowledge, love, and wisdom must now inhabit a body that has yet to learn to walk, talk, and take its rightful place in the physical world. There is much confusion at first. A soul senses. A body thinks. A soul floats. A body walks. A soul is timeless. A body ages. A soul has no boundaries. A body has physical limits.

In a short time span—a concept foreign to the timeless soul—a child must begin to integrate his basic physical and nonphysical parts and use them together to form his unique perspective, individuality, and purpose here on earth. And his first attempts at combining these parts occur while interacting with his family.

The Family as a Learning Place

"I just want my parents to listen to me."

"If only they would stop trying to make me be them and let me find my own way."

"Why don't they understand that I can take care of my-self?"

"No matter how I try, they just don't want to hear what I have to say."

"They don't give me any credit. They don't think I know anything!"

When a child enters a family, either by birth or by choice, he adds his own unique blend of spirituality and physical abilities to the mix. Adults, having spent more time on the physical planet, are helpful in teaching children how to adapt and learn in the physical world. Children, having spent more recent time on a spiritual level, remind adults of a timeless connection to the spiritual world and its love and wisdom. This shared learning has nothing to do with being bigger or better, older or younger, but is based on knowledge, wisdom, potential, intelligence, and love.

"Cindy is just like her father. The minute she was born she acted exactly like him. She's her father's daughter. That's a fact. They understand each other. They just know how they feel. Tim, my older son, is just like Scott, his brother. They're like mirrors. They've got each other's number. They know just how to get under each other's skin in a minute. My little one, Maggie, she loves her grandmother. It's as if she was born into the wrong family. Gramma can do no wrong in her book. There's always something going on in this family."

We are not born into our families by accident, whether the families are extended, single parent, adoptive, or foster care. People have spiritual connections or bonds with one or more family members. They are kindred souls, knowing each other on a spiritual level more deeply. Each member of a family brings to the family unit his talents, potential, and loving. The family becomes an intimate setting for mutual learning and support for every member. A great-grandfather can learn from an infant and an adolescent can learn from a sibling. Daily interactions between parents, children, and other relatives create situations where all may learn and teach those around them. A small child learning independence may enable a parent to express unconditional love more freely. A musically gifted child may encourage a relative to explore long-neglected artistic abilities. Each member of a family grows through shared experience, adding wealth to the living unit. When viewed this way, the family is more than a haphazard group of people thrown together with problems that one must endure until one can be legally independent. It becomes a fertile place of learning for both adults and children, creating conflict and resolution that can benefit both body and soul.

Certainly no family is perfect. A growing organism, it is a hothouse for change. A place where individuals in various stages of development share and grow, it can provide insight and support as well as conflict, friction, and blindness. Combative situations may become catalysts for change, understanding, compassion, and independence. There can also be resolve, loving, and growth at any time within the family unit.

Within one family, bodies may resemble each other and share physical likes and dislikes. There is a shared chronological and genealogical history among members. There are also souls who are alike in development. For no logical reason, a daughter may feel closer to a father whom she does not physically resemble. A mother may feel close to two children out of five, although she loves them all. An adopted child may feel instantly close to a grandmother or sibling. A stepfather may feel a greater kinship with a stepchild than with his own birth child. They are connected to each other more deeply as souls than as bodies.

Siblings may bond more closely with one than with another on a soul level even though in everyday life they may have more in common with other brothers or sisters. There may be family members who have built emotional defenses around themselves and are at odds most of the time because they touch each other deeply. Whether these spiritual bonds are recognized or rejected, they remain constant in the lives of those involved. These special timeless ties do not go away no matter how anyone tries to ignore or destroy them. Soul bonds prevail more deeply than physical family history and are nonverbal and deeply felt. Some examples are:

- The brothers who feuded all their lives and then found their loving connection when a parent died.
- The grandmother who felt deeper emotion for her grandchild than for her own son.
- The mother who chose the least likely child in the family to live with in her old age.

These timeless connections join people to each other without logical reason.

A child's physical place in the family hierarchy may also help his soul's specific learning. A middle child may need to develop diplomacy and sharing and teach patience to a parent who was a firstborn child. The youngest child may need to develop independence while teaching a single parent how to let go. An older sister may be more emotionally immature than a younger one, and two brothers may have completely different connections with each parent even though they may be only a year apart in age. Each soul wants to share its unique potential. With different sizes, ages, and levels of growing, each member comes to the family to develop his or her innate spiritual and physical attributes.

Some people believe families not only have soul connections among members but also may have shared previous lives with one another. A father may have been a brother with a son in a previous life. A sister may have been a mother to another sibling in another life. These karmic connections may psychologically enhance the current bonds between family members while encouraging new experiences to cherish and share.

People of many different cultures look forward to the advent of children not only in their own families but also in other families within the larger community. In parts of Africa, families name babies based on specific powers they hope will be of special significance in their lives. People often say, "Children are gifts of God that are simply lent to us." Each child enters the human family at his own level of growing. His potential is within him. His living road map is an integral part of his makeup. Parents may physically nurture and influence him, but he comes into this world with his own special talents, hopes, and loving to develop, use, and share. Physically inexperienced at first, he may become more practically adept than his elders. He may be more musically or athletically inclined than other family members. He may solve mathematical problems his parents could never fathom. He may be unafraid to take chances and be a natural leader while other relations make fewer inroads in life. Often parents will say, "I don't know where he gets his ideas. His courage. His talents. He's not like anyone else in the family." Each child brings his unique blueprint to the family and puts his imprint on others.

When family members understand that their living experience consists of many levels, both spiritual and physical, they can begin to appreciate each person as a special source and addition to the unit. Without the physical hierarchy imposed by culture and living, there can be more sharing and learning. An older body may learn from a young body with an old soul. A parent may teach a child how to save money and a child may teach a parent how to save time. A child may be frustrated trying to shoot basketball like his older brother but he may be the only one to enable his brother to show his deepest affection. Respect for each family member, regardless of age or size, allows everyone in the family to benefit greatly.

A parent must remember that an old soul in a young body who demonstrates incredible maturity or acts with empathy well beyond his years sometimes just wants an extra cookie for dessert to make him happy. Although children are looked upon as simple reminders of our physical innocence, they are unique souls here to fulfill their own potential. It is often said that "the child is father of Man." In some instances it is true. The family is the first experience for any child in a lifelong journey in the physical world. It is where children begin to learn about and use their spiritual potential and their physical attributes. The family, with its bumps and bruises, touching moments, and shared history, can be a dynamic catalyst toward the full realization of all its members.

Common Questions and Answers

Are all children more spiritually advanced than adults?

Each person brings into the world his or her own spiritual talents. Some children will be older and wiser souls than some adults, while some adults will be more spiritually developed than the children or adults around them. Differences in development do not depend on age but on the individual and his living connection to the spiritual level.

Are children more able to sense their souls than adults?

Children are usually more consciously aware of and naturally more comfortable with their souls than adults. This does not mean that children are more spiritually evolved than adults. It simply means that children are closely allied with their souls because they have had fewer years of living in the physical world. They naturally rely more on their souls as they develop physically, while adults have had more time to build psychological or physical defenses that may limit their natural spiritual focus. Many adults have retained the intuitive child within and relate to their souls as easily as children.

How can we help children to maintain their soul connection while their bodies grow?

Encourage a child to develop and feel good about his intuitive abilities and his soul's special attributes—his creativity, his unconditional loving, his deeper sense of connection to life—and he will maintain his connection with his soul and feel comfortable appreciating his body and soul in daily ways.

Is there a difference between being male or female when developing body and soul? Is it better to be male or female in a family learning situation?

Learning is based on individual potential and growth rather than gender. However, in Western culture boys are often trained to rely on the physical aspects of living: logical thinking, physical strength and talents, and attaining physical goals. Girls are encouraged to develop their intuitive senses and to focus on creativity, long-range plans, and dreams. But despite a girl's or boy's being steered in a specific direction, learning ability is specific to the individual. There is no better or more powerful sex.

How can children work on their physical and spiritual development if parents are not focused on their own development or are emotionally, sexually, or physically destructive?

Family situations are often filled with conflict and adversity. If his parents remain blocked to their own potential, a child may become more defensive or develop his own psychological defenses for added security. He may search beyond the immediate family and seek support from those with whom he has a spiritual bond—a grandfather, neighbor, or teacher. Some children grow in a positive way despite adverse family situations. Others are victimized and limited by them. With the support of the people around them, children can continue to develop despite self-destructive tendencies of any family members.

Is it better for a child to develop the attributes of his soul or his body?

There are many people who consider intellectual growth the normal goal. Others value developing the soul over developing physical attributes. Every part of a child needs to grow to enable him to become a whole person. A child who develops only spiritually disassociates himself from the physical world. A child focused only on developing physically denies his deeper connection to others and the use of his creative and intuitive talents. Both sets of attributes are essential to achieve balance and potential.

Are children more aware of the universal connection between us all?

Children may be verbally unaware of our universal connection, but they are naturally comfortable in reminding us of its existence. They love indiscriminately and empathize willingly. They forgive and accept our biggest foibles, reminding us by example that such loving exists.

Whenever five-year-old Kenisha was sad she talked to her imaginary friend, Pete. He would tell her things while they played together. One day a neighbor came to visit Kenisha's mother with her sister-in-law, who was visiting from another state. While her mother was getting them coffee Kenisha started telling them about Pete. She described him and told them all about his toys and his favorite room. As she went into great detail the neighbor looked at her sister-in-law in shock. The boy Kenisha was describing was an exact match for Peter, the sister-in-law's son, who had died of meningitis at age four—ten years before Kenisha was born.

Sean was born three years after his grandmother died. When he was eight years old his grandmother came to him in a dream. In the dream she was standing in front of his bed. She told him that she had given his mother a gold watch for him that had been her own father's. She told him to ask his mother about Paddy's gold watch. In the morning Sean did as instructed. Taken aback, his mother asked him how he knew about it. Sean told her about his grandmother and described her perfectly. His mother told him that she had been saving her great-grandfather's gold watch, given to her by her mother before she died, for him in her safe deposit box at the bank.

Second-grader Noriko was at home, sick. While her mother fed her soup, Noriko began telling her about a picnic by a lake. "You and Daddy and me were there. Just us," she offered. "It was in California." Her mother looked at Noriko in surprise, since she had lived all of her short life in New York. "Why do you say this, Noriko?" her mother asked. "Is it because you know your Daddy and I lived in California before you were born?" "No," Noriko insisted. "I remember when you walked up to the top of the mountain and you had *to be carried down because you got sick. I was sick then, too." Noriko's mother recalled that in the seventh month of her pregnancy, she and Noriko's father had eaten beside a lake and then hiked up a small mountain in Northern California. She had suddenly become ill and had to be carried down the mountain. This minor incident had never been discussed with Noriko and her mother had forgotten all about it until now.*

<u>3</u>

Invisible Friends and Visitors

In childhood magical things can occur.

Stories read aloud become alive. Games and activities turn vivid and real. Everyday journeys are adventures that are larger than life. Toys and invisible friends are alive, and they are constant loving companions.

It is a time when anything can happen.

Imaginary Friends

Adult: "Who are you talking to?"
Child: "My invisible friend."
Adult: "What's his name?"
Child: "Rusty."
Adult: "What does Rusty do?"
Child: "He plays with me and tells me things."
Adult: "How come I can't see him?"
Child: "Because you're not looking."

This special communication between spirit or soul friends and children has been evident throughout human history and commonly continues today. Many adults can recall speaking to imaginary friends in their childhood—friends they once played with and loved, and then forgot. Mental thinking explains away these experiences as figments of young imaginations, a psychological means of helping a child overcome the loss of a loved one or compensation for certain social skills that are lacking.

In some cases that might be absolutely true. But what if in other instances these special playmates actually are present? And children really see and converse with them? Are these children unbalanced? Or are they simply seeing something adults have learned to forget?

When most adults recall their childhood experiences with their imaginary friends they always smile and feel happy. They remember these friends as quite real and their experiences with them as special. Most adults remember their names.

Having spent less time living in the physical world, children are more keenly aware of their spiritual connections. They know what it feels like to be a spirit or soul. Children may see blue or white spirit lights floating in the dark, auras of colored light surrounding trees or people or the spirits of deceased loved ones without being afraid. That reality is not foreign to them. They have come to our physical world recently. And this life is more foreign to them at this moment in their development.

In China, those children with the ability to see spirits are said to have been born with "yin/yang eyes" able to see the active world of the living as well as the passive world of the dead. In rural areas of the Scottish Highlands children seek out fairies and elfin people to teach them games and daily tasks. They are comfortable having "the little people" accompany them in doing whatever they do. They welcome them.

Since children have not learned to block their nonphysical

perceptions and knowledge psychologically, they are more visually aware of things closely aligned with their souls. It is natural and ordinary for a child to play as easily with a nonphysical friend as with a physical one. Prejudice against anyone or anything is learned. To a child, any close friend, whether physical or nonphysical, is cherished and loved despite noticeable differences.

Spirit friends are not just casual acquaintances chosen at random; they have deep spiritual connections with the children. These kindred spirits, often referred to as guides, guardian angels, or guardian spirits, are very old and dear special friends. They may be as old as the child's soul and may serve to guide the child, whether visibly or invisibly, throughout the child's adult life. On a spiritual level, they and the child continue to know and love each other as the child matures physically.

A spirit friend, like any other good friend, will be helpful and supportive but not interfere with the child's life. A confidant, he will help guide the child in his learning and will love the child and protect him from danger and harm. In exchange the spirit friend shares in the child's physical experience and growth.

In many Native American tribes, children consciously meet their spirit friends or guardian spirits during rites of passage into adulthood. Guardian spirits are also common to tribes in South America and in parts of Australia, Melanesia, and Africa. As they approach adulthood, male children of the Plains tribes and both male and female members of other North American tribes undergo physical training to meet their guardian spirits—a process culminating in vision quests. During a vision quest, a child goes to a solitary place, fasts for four days, and in a dream or waking state seeks the presence of a guardian spirit who will remain with him for the rest of his life. This spirit may appear to him in visions or dreams in the form of an elk, wolf, bear, eagle, buffalo, or other animal. The guardian spirit teaches the child its sacred song to be used to call upon him in times of need. A guardian spirit is a benevolent teacher and source of protection for the child during his entire life.

Modern children of many cultures are also likely to encounter their spirit friends for the first time in dreams. While dreaming, the physical body is at rest and free from distraction. Upon waking, the child who remains in touch with the "other side" continues the same active level of loving communication with his newly rediscovered friend. The feelings are heartfelt and the communication is always mutual. No intrusion or force is involved.

Children are usually spontaneously happy and excited to communicate with their spirit friends. Comfortable with the encounter, they openly share their experiences, confidences, information, joy, and general sense of communion with these special soul friends. Often able to "see" their imaginary playmates in physical form, children acutely know when they are present and intuitively communicate with them, often identifying them by sound or name.

Some children actively "hear" their imaginary playmates and converse with them. Others sense them. When asked how their imaginary friends speak to them, they reply, "I just know her voice" or "He talks to me inside my head," referring to telepathic communication, the most comfortable form of mutual intuitive communication. Even when children cannot hear or see their imaginary playmates they sense their presence and feel their active loving support around them.

When not taught to fear or reject this friendship, children continue to communicate with their imaginary friends while they learn to become physically focused. Serving almost as a bridge between the spirit world and the physical world, an imaginary friend helps a child's soul as it adjusts to its new physical environment. Old friends never disappear. Like true guardian angels they remain nearby whether they are physically perceived or never seen.

How adults treat the existence of imaginary friends plays a special part in a child's healthy acceptance or rejection of his spiritual life. If an adult rejects the possibility of a child's soul friend, the child may consciously turn away from his intuitive talents and look upon them with disdain or fear. Seeking adult approval, a child may become unsure of his perceptions and feelings, and follow a parent's wishes or fears.

In a world where physical senses rule, adults become wary that prolonged contact with imaginary playmates may make a child less reality oriented, socially conscious, or emotionally balanced. Yet adults who speak of experiences with their own childhood imaginary friends share none of these problems. They invariably smile and recount those times as happy, sweet, loving, and special.

For any adult who knows a child who communicates with an imaginary playmate, it is important to remember that the child can sense your true approval or disapproval as you are speaking to him. Try to remain neutral and open so that the child can be allowed the freedom to explore his personal experiences. If a child becomes increasingly emotionally attached to an imaginary playmate during times of stress (family problems, loss of a loved one, and so on), keep an open mind and encourage him to communicate freely with others as well about what he is feeling.

An adult who is included in these special experiences may find them enlightening. With time and awareness, that adult may even realize that the child and his spirit guide have become a bridge for reconnecting to his own spiritual impressions.

Dreams and Nightmares

Imaginary friends are just one aspect of the dream life of children. Especially sensitive children may also see or visit with deceased loved ones, gain priceless wisdom and information, and see events in the future.

In Siberia children who foresee the future in their dreams are recognized for their positive talents and trained to become future shamans, or Nga. Using information gained from their intuitive dreaming, they help cure the sick, divine the future, and protect the well-being of their people.

> *"Mommy, I had a dream that Daddy and you and me went to the playground and we bought ice cream. And Sarah was there. And we bought her ice cream, too."*

In this dream the child is drawing on her recent past experiences, having been to the playground with her parents and having seen Sarah with her parents in the supermarket the day before. Such dreams are ways in which the body releases physical information, emotional impressions, and experiences. They are called working-through dreams and can usually be traced to physical events, relationships, and situations the child has recently experienced. The body clears the brain of information it no longer needs and the process is sometimes remembered upon awakening. An adult can logically trace a child's tangible sources so as to understand the derivation of his dream. Working-through dreams are abundant for everyone of every age and may or may not be remembered upon awakening.

> *"I went to a place where there were cars that flew in the sky but they weren't like our cars. They just moved like air-*

*planes but higher. I think that's the way we're going to drive
in a few years."*

Other dreams differ from working-through dreams. They
often have no physical explanation and do not relate to any past
or recent daily experiences. These dreams are spiritual in nature.
They are known as intuitive dreams and are often referred to as
visions. Not usually experienced on a continual basis, these
dreams do not adhere to any set structure or time but often give
information, insight, and communication to enrich our lives.
They can happen for anyone at any time in his life. Unlike mental dreaming, these dreams are unusually clear and vivid and
they last in memory long after we awaken. An intuitive dream
may be recalled in colorful detail, invoking strong feelings or
images the next day or even years later.

Still naturally attuned to their spiritual nature, children are
often clearly aware of their dreams. Since their physical minds
have not been conditioned to block information psychologically
upon awakening, their dream life is abundant and perceptions
are very real and vivid.

Strong impressions of the future, visions of places and colors,
communication with or sensing of loved ones who have passed
on, and spiritual comfort given to help in current situations may
be so vividly rich that the dreamer is stimulated to talk about
them. The dream may be so evocative it even wakes him from
sleep. The vision may seem so real that upon awakening a child
momentarily loses his sense of his physical surroundings and becomes frightened. Unable at first to relate the dream sensations
verbally, he may panic or cry. Once his body is comforted he will
return to his natural cycle of sleep.

When a child is emotionally upset after dreaming, he can immediately sense others' reactions. Resentment or fear from an
adult can heighten his distress. So allow him time to rebalance.

Hold him. Talk to him. Let him feel the physical comfort of your body. Once he is calm, encourage him to talk about his dream, or if he is tired or unwilling, discuss it with him in the morning. By verbalizing his dream impressions he can work through his feelings of isolation and fear. Positive interest in learning about his dreams enables him to see them as normal experiences.

The way we view dreams and the way we receive spiritual information has a lot to do with what our culture teaches us. An interesting study, done for the Bureau of Psychology of the state of Uttar Pradesh, India, by Jamunda Prasad and Ian Stevenson in 1962–63, showed how cultural differences affect the way children deal with their dreams. Children in the United States and children in India with similar intuitive talents were observed.

It was discovered that visions of the future commonly occur in dreams for Western children while those same experiences occur during waking states in Indian children. Openly receptive to active intuitive communication and spiritual experiences, the Indian culture frees children to discuss and share their dream perceptions as natural and daily parts of their lives. Western children, culturally taught to repress their intuitive perceptions, frequently only experience them when their conscious minds are at rest.

If a child is encouraged to talk about his dreams at an early age, he will feel free to integrate his dream state and other spiritual experiences comfortably into his daily life. He will also more consciously distinguish between working-through dreams and intuitive dreams. Treating dreams as natural adventures that are new and fun will help a child to know that when he lies down to sleep a special experience awaits him.

"I was flying. I could see all the trees. And then I saw Gramma in a big house and she told me she was happy. She was holding my hand so I wouldn't be afraid."

Children frequently describe such dream experiences as "flying." They remember flying above rooftops and treetops, and even above the stars, without wings or mechanical aid. Unaware of their bodies, they feel unusually light, floating just like a soul outside a body. Children generally enjoy these experiences, excited about flying and other out-of-body trips. They may fly above ground, visit homes of friends or relatives, see spirit guides or loved ones, or find themselves looking down with curious interest at their bodies asleep in their beds.

Sometimes they return to their bodies too abruptly after such an experience, and then their bodies may momentarily be jarred by the sudden return of their souls. Quickly awakened by the experience, and not knowing what happened, the children may become nervous or frightened. It may take a moment for their nerves to settle down again and for them to regain their balance. When such experiences happen, adults can recount some of their own flying dreams or remind children that what they are experiencing will pass, that they do not have to feel frightened, and remain with them until their equilibrium returns.

In their intuitive dreams, children may also revisit spiritual levels to connect with other souls. This form of movement is called out-of-body travel or astral projection, a natural experience everyone shares during sleep whether we remember it or not. It is often a way for our spirits to help recharge our bodies, give us useful information and spiritual energy, or enable us to communicate with guides or loved ones solely on the spiritual level. Upon awakening, a child will often relate a spiritual message or insight from a loved one whose death may or may not have been recent. These instances are not unusual. In many cultures such spiritual meetings with the dead are even encouraged. In rural Japan, children are given specific instructions about communication with ancestor souls. Conversations with deceased ancestors are experienced as ordinary parts of their lives.

In Africa, ancestor worship and communication are part of tradition. Children in the West Indies, Brazil, and Puerto Rico, schooled in intuitive traditions, actively participate with family members in séances where there is conscious group communication with souls. Those children who show exceptional psychic talents in spiritual communication are encouraged to develop these talents at very young ages.

When a person physically dies his soul continues living on a spiritual level. Soon after his physical death he may return to family members and friends left behind to give them comfort during their grieving, let them know he loves them, and remind them he may be physically apart but is spiritually still close to them. A child naturally open to the spiritual level may see or sense the deceased person's presence in or around the house. He may describe or feel the deceased loved one, whom he may not previously have known, and give information about that person with uncanny accuracy.

Visitations from loved ones are usually emotionally touching; but during times of grief and loss they may be momentarily disconcerting for others, producing upset, fear, or bittersweet feelings. A child may be taken by surprise by the emotional reactions of others when relating what is a natural experience for him. Simply assure him that he is not responsible for others' reactions. Do not force him to continue communicating with the deceased loved one if he does not desire to do so. His words or impressions should be acknowledged and not judged. Let his information serve as proof of a visitation. If allowed to integrate his spiritual and physical experiences naturally, a child will have a well-rounded view of life and of physical death.

If a child becomes fearful during any visitation experience, give him emotional support and comfort and ask the loved one to leave. Doing this enables the loved one to be aware of his soul's effect on the energy of the child and helps the child to see that his life is within his control. Loved ones, not wanting to disturb but rather to comfort, will instantly leave and can return at any time that is mutually decided.

If a child still feels fearful after nightly visitations from a friendly soul:

• Set aside time before going to sleep to read him a story he loves and enjoy it with him.

• Laugh with him and discuss the events of the next day so he can relax before sleeping.

• While you are with the child, audibly ask the friendly visitor not to visit during the night.

The child's body may simply need some time to trust and become accustomed to sleeping undisturbed again. After a full night of undisturbed dreams, his body will return to its normal pattern of sleep.

"Mommy! There was a big man chasing me! He was angry and I couldn't run away! I didn't know who he was!"

There may be many causes why a child has difficulty sleeping or is extremely fearful or agitated when sent to bed. He may continuously cry himself to sleep or call out for a parent in the middle of the night. Psychological or physical problems need to be addressed and rectified. But there may be other causes that disturb him that have no physiological derivation. For some children, unwanted visitations during sleep do occur.

Nightmares can be the result of working-through dreams stemming from a child's physical or psychological problems or fears. With open communication and/or professional help a child's sleep pattern can be restored. Other nightmares may originate from a completely different source. The energy of a deceased person unknown to the family might disturb a child's body. This soul may appear to a child vividly in dreams or as a sensed presence in the room, causing the child to awaken and feel fearful. This soul is not intent on harming the child. It is simply misdirected, or its energy may be out of balance. The sensitive child is affected on a spiritual level, and inadvertently this discomfort affects the child's body and causes a physical reaction.

> *A child is walking down a familiar street. Walking down the same street after having just had an argument with her husband, a stranger seems upset when she realizes she is lost. As the stranger nears the child to ask for directions, the child intuitively senses the stranger's agitation and feels uncomfortable around her. The child's intuitive reaction is to avoid her. Something does not feel right. However, the stranger continues to innocently approach the child because she needs to find out where she is. Although she has no intention of harming the child, her misdirected energy upsets the child enough to cause the child to feel alarmed even though there may be many other strangers walking down the same street.*

On a spiritual level similar encounters may occur. This stranger, or "confused soul," may inadvertently have lost its way and may be unable to find its proper direction or the person it is seeking. Just as the stranger on the street did not mean to frighten or upset the child, neither does the confused soul. Both the stranger and the confused soul are unaware of their effect on the child. Since such visitations are more likely to occur when a child is sleeping and his body is at rest, the encounter may be frightening in the moment, and the child may describe it as a nightmare.

An isolated nightmare of this kind is usually remedied. Frightened by the presence of a confused soul, the child's body awakens and the confused soul generally moves on. The child's body begins to quiet and resumes a peaceful sleep. If his body is fearful of returning to sleep, afraid that the same confused soul may return, he may need some tangible comfort: a warm glass of milk, a reassuring adult to remain in the room until he falls asleep again. The child may even feel apprehensive about falling asleep for several nights until he is physically sure the disturbed soul will not visit again.

Some children's sleep patterns regularly become disturbed. The children may sleep well for weeks and then have a series of sleepless nights or fearful nightmares. In many instances this is due to psychological fears or emotional trauma a child may be physically experiencing and should be addressed through psychological or physical means. In other incidences it may be due to visitations by confused souls unknown to the child. Such children who experience these visitations are very intuitively sensitive. They are finely attuned to the presence of any souls around them, especially when their bodies are at rest and not physically distracted and focused.

When such nightmares occur with regularity there are several things that can be done to help an intuitive child return to normal sleep:

• Allow the child to verbalize his impressions and feelings no matter how bizarre or fearful or ridiculous they may sound.

• Encourage him to talk about his whole dream so that psychological, emotional, and spiritual factors may be noted. Through verbalization he will be able to externalize his experience instead of turning his fears inward. An adult will be able to uncover the causes for his sleep discomfort more readily with more information at hand.

• If his fears frighten others around him in the family let him know you are with him in this experience and he is not alone. Hold him and let him feel your physical support so that he can restore his calm and balance. Talking honestly about your own childhood nightmares and feelings will enable him to understand that others have similar experiences.

• If what he says is confusing, ask him specific questions. This will help him focus and look logically at any of his irrational fears. Feeling safe, he may be more willing to talk about his feelings to gain insight and understanding.

• His fears may seem imaginary but his feelings are very real to him and at the moment very disturbing. Hold him, touch him, allow him to feel your body beside him, and reassure him that your love for him will not disappear.

• If his body is too stimulated for sleep, he can dispel excessive tensions by shaking his hands vigorously and sending "bad feelings" away from his body and out of the room. Stay nearby until he becomes sleepy. Leave a night light on so that he will not feel isolated by the dark.

• If in the following nights the child continues to resist bedtime out of a fear of nightmares, spend time with him before he prepares for bed. Talk about positive plans for the next day. If he strongly resists going to sleep, help him find an imaginary friend who will look after him through the night. Place a picture or a keepsake from a loved one near his pillow to give him a physical contact with someone he wants to watch over him.

• If he is aware of a spirit friend or has a favorite stuffed animal or doll, make sure that his special friend is with him before he goes to bed. In Guatemala children are sometimes encouraged to put several little dolls under their pillow when they sleep. The child tells these "worry dolls" his worries or problems before going to bed and then sleeps with them during the night. In the morning the dolls are retrieved, having worked through the night to take the child's worries away. Finding the doll in the morning is a pleasant and tangible reminder for a child that there has been positive help during the night. A child will, as he regains trust in himself, naturally become less reliant on outside help or comfort for his own inner balance.

If the confused soul persists in making its presence known to the child there are other possibilities for helping to ensure peaceful sleep:

• Since children are very visual, help the child visualize the person he fears. Let him talk to his vision in your presence.

• If he is afraid to speak, ask the vision questions and let the child relate his answers to you. This will accustom the child to its presence in a safe atmosphere and allow him to feel his own power and relax.

• Tell the confused soul that it must go away and find help, and not frighten the child. This will allow the confused soul to gain knowledge and regain its own stability as well as help the child face his fears. By feeling the power to confront and remedy problems a child will feel more capable of controlling situations.

• If a child is unwilling to speak to or visualize the confused soul, ask him to imagine a special friendly "monster" who is bigger and benign and who can deal with the confused soul. Ask the friendly monster to talk to the confused soul and make it go away.

• Ask the friendly monster to color the confused soul in friendly colors of the child's choosing that will make it less scary.

• Imagine the confused soul and dress it in clothing that will be less threatening, like a clown suit or a baby bonnet. Once a child feels comfortable with this exercise, his feelings about the episode may change and be more positive and productive.

• Let him ask his angel, or an invisible friend or deceased loved one, to take the confused soul to a place far away from his sleeping place. Knowing the confused soul is in good hands, a child will feel less apprehensive.

• If you have exhausted all outlets, both physical and spiritual, and a child still continues to have severe sleep disturbances, he may need to see a trained medium or channeler experienced in soul communication. A professional medium, just like a trained doctor, can assess the situation on a spiritual level using his or her talents to communicate directly with the confused soul and help remedy the situation. Knowing that something that appears frightening can be remedied eases a child's fears on all levels and allows him to feel safe again to experience his dreams positively.

Common Questions and Answers

Does an imaginary playmate stay with you when you become an adult?

Imaginary playmates or spirit guides are old friends. Like other old friends, they stay close to you throughout your life, sharing with and caring for you. They are always there and willing to help you no matter what your age.

Does everyone have a spirit friend or spirit guide?

Everyone has more than one spirit friend, just as everyone has more than one physical friend or person with whom he or she is close. These nonphysical friends grow along with you, and even though they may not be physically present, they continue to help and love and remain close to your soul. There are also occasions when a loved one who has died decides to help guide those with whom he still feels closely bonded. Such souls work closely with a person's soul and his other soul friends in loving ways.

If a child does not recognize his spirit friend when he is young, will he be less intuitive in later life than a child who does see his spirit friend?

Children who see their spirit friends at young ages are already showing signs of using and trusting their natural intuitive abilities. If a child does not see or sense souls or a spirit friend, it is not a measure of his intuitive talents. He may be more intuitively talented in other ways; he may be more capable of communicating telepathically or able to feel future impressions about people or events. Knowing a spirit friend is simply one of the ways children remain connected to the nonphysical or spiritual part of themselves.

Are spirit friends dangerous? Can seeing them open a child to possible visitations by confused souls?

Whether a child recognizes a spirit friend or not, such souls are always there as loving friends. A spirit friend's energy is very compatible to the energy of the child's soul and cannot be dangerous because the bond is lovingly close and enduring. A child may come across a confused soul at any time in his life without knowing it. He may be momentarily disturbed in his dreams (although certainly not all disturbances are caused by confused souls) or have his energy balance disturbed even when he is conscious. It is usually his spirit friend who helps protect the child by trying to aid the confused soul to regain its balance and move on. The child's spirit friend is always there to help the child's soul maintain its natural equilibrium.

How can you tell the difference between a child's natural imagination and what he may be experiencing intuitively?

It may at times be difficult to distinguish between a child's imaginative thinking, the daily experiences that stimulate him, and his intuitive impressions and experiences. Allowing a child the freedom to express anything he is feeling or seeing will enable you to see what may possibly be intuitively oriented. As a child learns to discuss his experiences openly, certain patterns and descriptions will emerge that will clearly define the obvious differences for you.

How can you tell if a confused soul is really gone? Will it ever return to bother the child?

You can tell when a confused soul is gone by the way the child is behaving. After several moments, an hour, an evening, or even a few days, the child's natural ways and actions should reassert themselves. It may take a little while for his body to trust that those feelings that scared him will not return, to balance his energies, and to restore his harmony. A confused soul, once aware of its effect on the child, will usually be open to receiving nonphysical direction or help; it will balance its energies and will not return again. If a child is still having nightmares and experiences that indicate possible visitations by a confused soul, practice some of the suggestions offered earlier in this chapter or seek the counsel of an experienced medium.

If a loved one has died, and his energy has left his body, why would he come back to the physical world?

The soul of a deceased family member or loved one is not trying to be physical. It is visiting the people it loves to let them know it is present in a nonphysical dimension. Such souls may come to reassure or comfort a grieving person, especially if the deceased person died suddenly and was unable to say good-bye. A loved one may also revisit, either on a conscious level or through dreams, to communicate something or to help someone with an immediate problem. A loved one who has a strong bond with another person will always be available to love and comfort him on many levels beyond a physical way of being.

4

Intuitive Exercises
and Games

All children are naturally intuitive but not all children share the same types of intuitive or psychic talents. There are eight distinctly different types of intuitive talents used by children: Intuitive Reading, Psychometry Reading, Aura Reading, Intuitive Healing, Clairvoyance, Psychokinesis and Levitation, Mediumship, and Telepathy. In this chapter, the types of intuitive talents are discussed individually, each with specific exercises for children to practice.

Some children are extremely talented in one intuitive area. Others easily combine several talents. No one intuitive talent is better to have than another. Each child can learn to develop his own spiritual potential.

Immediate and positive results are possible for any exercise, but the most important goal is the child's discovery of intuitive talents. Do not pressure the child to perform or to compete with others while practicing his intuitive talents. Group exercises are meant to be shared. None of the exercises is a test of his psychic talents. Instead, each one is a means of exploring his potential. Let him repeat any exercise and reject others according to his desires. He may create new exercises or improvise on those already tried. They are stepping stones to help him feel comfortable using his natural abilities. Less emphasis on structure and more on fun will allow him to discover his abilities at his own natural pace.

Let his desire to learn lead him. Children do not differentiate between their natural talents when using them, so let him have fun. Try several exercises. Design your own.

Primary Exercises

Primary exercises can be practiced before any psychic exercises to calm, relax, and focus children. These handy exercises, once learned, can be used during any part of a child's day to help him with other tasks, tests, and experiences at home or in the classroom. He can use them before doing homework, to get a good night's sleep, before an athletic activity or a test, in an emotional situation, or just for all-around well-being.

Releasing Tension

Releasing Tension is a conscious way for a child to let go of any excessive energy he may have accumulated throughout his day. It can be used anytime and anyplace, whenever a child needs to focus on an activity: if he is too stimulated to sleep, distracted in class, nervous or apprehensive before a test, emotionally upset. Practiced in the home, at school, in a restaurant, or on the playing field, it enables a child to feel more comfortable emotionally and physically.

Try any of the following exercises or interchange them, depending on which your child finds most fun or comfortable.

RELEASING TENSION EXERCISES

1. Place your hands on an object:
   - The sides of a chair
   - The desk at school
   - The bed
   - A favorite toy or blanket
   - Anything that is not living

   And place your feet on:
   - The floor
   - A mattress
   - The floor of the car

Let all nervousness or tension move from your body through your hands and feet into the floor or object.
Feel the energy leaving you.
Review what you feel during and after the exercise.

2. While standing or seated shake your hands very hard in the air.
   Send all energy and tension away from your body.
   Do it as long as you like and as often as you wish.

3. Visualize a great big balloon attached to a basket.
   Put your problem into the basket and send the balloon away.
   Watch it move out of the room and out of sight.

4. Look at a big fluffy cloud or a star.
   Send your worries to the cloud or star and watch them move away.

5. See a nice comfortable place like a beach or rock or tree.
   Imagine yourself right there and relax.
   Feel all your problems fall away from you and disappear.

Releasing Tension can be done any way, at any time for as long as a child wants to use it. Try different ways and see what is felt during and after the tensions are released.

Relaxation

Relaxation is fun for children because they use their natural sense of creativity and curiosity. After doing a Releasing Tension exercise, or if a child simply wishes to relax and feel calm, Relaxation can be used to help maintain energy for balance and focus.

RELAXATION EXERCISE

1. Listen to your breathing. What does it sound like? Is it fast? Slow?

   Feel your breath in your nose, your throat, your chest.

   Feel your breath in your tummy.

   Send your breath down to your hips, your legs, feet, and toes.

   Fill your whole self with your breathing and listen.

   Now quicken your breath. What does it feel like?

   Slow down your breathing. What do you feel?

   Send all your breath to your feet. What do you feel?

   Send all your breath to your hands. What do you feel?

2. Picture a beautiful light or a color around the outside of your head.

   Take that light and cover your whole body with it like a blanket.

3. Bring a beautiful light of color inside your body and breathe it into your chest, then your belly, your arms and fingers, your legs and feet.

Let the beautiful light grow outside your body and fill the whole room.

4. Now, tense your feet and breathe the light into them and relax them.

    Do the same with your legs. Tense them, breathe the light, and relax.

    Do the same with your stomach, chest, arms and hands, neck, and face.

    Check to make sure every part of your body is filled with light and relaxed. If not, breathe the light into that part and relax it.

These simple visual breathing exercises help children to discover their bodies, achieve balance, relax, and relate to their natural energy.

Feeling Response

A child's Feeling Response, located in his solar plexus, is the combination of a natural physical and intuitive response to every situation, person, and experience he encounters. These spontaneous feelings are objective and visceral. A Feeling Response can take either of two forms:

- A "yes" response, which may feel like a lightness in his stomach, a warmth, or an open happy feeling
- A "no" response, which may feel heavy, weighty, cold, tight, or closed down

A child gains confidence and self-esteem by trusting himself. Using his basic Feeling Response can help him make right decisions and build inner confidence. His Feeling Response has nothing to do with egotism or the exclusion of others. Listening to his inner voice will allow a child to make right decisions without denying himself in the process. Being aware of his Feeling Response can help a child quickly discover how valid his first impressions are in intuitive exercises and everyday life.

FEELING RESPONSE EXERCISE

Your "No" Feeling Response:
1. Put an open hand on your stomach (just above your navel) and think of someone or something you really do not like.

   What does it feel like? Does it feel warm? Cold? Uncomfortable? Happy?

   What is the real feeling in your stomach?

   Clear your mind and shake out your hand.

Your "Yes" Feeling Response:
2. Put your hand back on your stomach and think of someone or something you really love.

   What does it feel like? Does it feel warm? Cold? Uncomfortable? Happy?

   What is the real feeling in your stomach?

   Are the two feelings different?

3. Repeat the same exercise with other people or things or places.

   Find your Feeling Response.

   Are your "yes" responses the same?

   Are your "no" responses the same?

This Feeling Response exercise can be practiced anytime and anywhere. Children experiencing difficulty finding their Feeling

Response can practice Relaxation or Releasing Tension exercises, then try again.

4. Walk outside or in a mall or city block and stop beside a person or animal.
   See what your Feeling Response is for that person or animal.

5. At a restaurant choose what you want to eat using your Feeling Response.

6. If you are watching a television show or movie, use your Feeling Response to see what you feel about the characters in the movie or the people seated beside you in the room or theater.

7. Focus on someone in the morning and find your Feeling Response.
   Focus on the same person later on in the day and check for any differences.

8. Focus on a pet or a baby and find your Feeling Response.
   Focus on the pet or baby later on in the day and feel any differences.

9. Go to a food store and focus on different natural foods and find your Feeling Response. Any differences?

10. Draw a picture of people you know, coloring them with colors that fit your Feeling Response for them.
    Draw a picture of the same people at another time and see if their colors have changed based on your Feeling Response.

11. Look at pictures of relatives and friends or ads in a magazine and find your Feeling Response.

12. Choose a present for a birthday or special occasion for a family member or friend using your Feeling Response.

Intuitive Exercises and Games

A child may be a good dancer or he may excel at tap dancing but not do well at ballet. He may be a great athlete only on the basketball court. He may run a fast 440 in track and also excel at soccer. The same can be said of a child with intuitive talents. He may find one or two abilities easy to tap, but have difficulty with the others. Each of the eight types of abilities can be practiced initially to discover a child's intuitive or psychic skills.

No single intuitive ability is less or greater than any other. Children will spontaneously choose the abilities and exercises that interest them. In this way they will naturally be drawn to develop their own skills and talents in their own way and time.

None of the Intuitive Exercises and Games is based on or limited by physical age. Since old souls may live in young bodies, chronological age has little to do with psychic talents. Siblings and family members can participate in singular or group exercises at any time. Improvise upon any exercise, or create new exercises together.

HELPFUL TIPS FOR PARENTS

• Whenever the child feels tense or confused before, during, or after any intuitive exercise or game, have him practice Releasing Tension and Relaxation.

• Have the child practice Feeling Response to double-check any intuitive impression or information.

• The child should say any words, sentences, or thoughts that come into his mind during each exercise no matter how silly they may sound. They do not have to make sense or be in logical order; he should just say what comes into his mind.

• If he cannot do an exercise, help him relax. Practice any or all Primary Exercises and try again or go on to another exercise.

• Take your time with the exercises. See what happens.

• When doing a group exercise, let all the children practice Primary Exercises first.

• In group exercises allow enough time for everyone to get impressions. If there is writing involved, each person should place his pencil down as he finishes.

• If the child does not get any insights at first, try asking him some questions about what impressions he is feeling.

• If any information is wrong, have the child refocus and try again or try another exercise. Come back to the exercise later to show the child that he can also be right.

• The less information another person provides the easier it is for the child to gain insights.

• Make sure the child's body is comfortable for any exercise.

• Read the whole exercise through before trying it with the child.

- Remind the child to keep trying to get more words, colors, letters, energy in any exercise until there is no more coming to him.

- Skip around, practice whatever exercises the child wishes.

- Have fun!

Intuitive Reading

Intuitive Reading is being able to read the "vibes" of a person, animal, plant, tree, rock, or natural place and give thoughts impressions, words, feelings, descriptive pictures about them. Everybody has hunches. With Intuitive Reading we add words and ideas to our hunches.

Important: Remember to use your Feeling Response to tell if you are right.

INTUITIVE READING EXERCISES

1. When a family member or friend comes home, focus on him and see what impressions about him come to you:
   - Is he tired?
   - What kind of day did he have?
   - Who did he talk to?
   - What did he have for lunch?

   See if anything else pops into your head without asking. Make sure the other person lets you know if you are right!

   Reverse positions if you wish.

2. Read your teacher at school and privately say all your impressions to a school friend or family member.

   Read your teacher the next day and see if you get any other impressions.

3. Read a friend or a friend of a friend (someone you do not know well):
   - Where does his father or mother work?
   - How many brothers or sisters does he have?
   - What are they like?
   - What is the person's favorite food? Television show? Sport?

   Have someone who knows him tell you if you are right.

4. Keep a journal for a week, dating impressions about the people in your family:
   - What kind of day did they each have on Monday, Tuesday, and so on?
   - What did they eat for lunch each day?
   - What did they do at three o'clock?

   Check the results.

5. While watching a television game show or sports event sense the winner of the contest and the final score.

6. Read a baby or an animal and tell what the baby or animal will do in the next hour or afternoon.

7. Before watching a movie, predict what will happen. Then watch the movie.

8. Pick the fastest checkout person in the supermarket without looking.

9. If you are starting a new class or after-school activity, read your impressions about the instructor. See if you are right as you get to know the teacher better.

10. Group Exercise: Everyone choose one child to fill himself with an emotion—happy, sad, angry, silly, etc.—and each group member close his eyes and see what emotion he is feeling.

Change places until everyone gets a chance.

11. Group Exercise: Everyone choose one child to stand in front of the group.

Each member of the group should have a pencil and paper before him to write down impressions.

Everyone practice Releasing Tension then focus on the person and write down whatever impressions come into your mind. Keep writing until all impressions are written down.

Check each impression with your Feeling Response as you write it.

Do not put your name on the paper.

When all the pencils are down and everyone is finished have the person read the impressions and say if they are right.

Then choose another person to stand before the group and repeat the exercise.

Psychometry Reading

When we look at a photograph of a person or animal or hold an object that has been worn or owned by that person or animal we can get information about him. The person or animal does not have to be present. We can read his "vibes" from his picture or object just as we did with Intuitive Reading and get information about his past, present, or future.

The photograph or object does not have to be recent and it does not matter if the photograph is in color or black and white.

At first it might be better to read a photo of only one person. But a whole group of people can also be read.

Try not to use an object that was worn or handled by people other than the person focused upon. Their energies may confuse impressions being received.

PSYCHOMETRY READING EXERCISES

1. When choosing a present for someone, hold each selection in your hands separately and see what you feel about the item based on your psychic impressions.

   If you wish, clear your mind, and practice the Primary Exercises before you read each selection.

   Trust your Feeling Response when making your best choice.

2. Find a stone or leaf or shell or some other natural object and place it in the palm of your hand and see how old the object is, where it is from, where it has been, and so on.

3. Close your eyes and have another person select three choices of juice or cookies or CDs. They can place the choices in front of you or separately place each in your open hand, one at a time.

   See if you can sense impressions about each object: colors, musicians, taste.

   If the objects are before you, have the other person guide your hands over each without touching them.

   Say aloud all your impressions.

4. Have someone put an object inside a bag or box without telling you what it is.

   Say aloud all your impressions.

   Then check your results.

5. Have someone put three different liquids that look the same in glasses before you.

 Touch each glass with your eyes closed.

 Give your impression about each liquid.

 Taste them to see if you are right.

 Switch the order of the glasses and repeat the exercise.

6. Take an object from one of your parents and have another child do the same with one of his.

 With eyes closed, exchange the objects and give impressions about the object and the parent.

7. Have someone give you a cassette tape or CD. Without looking at it say all your impressions.
 * What type of music is on the CD?
 * Is the artist a male or female?
 * Is it a group?
 * What songs are on it?

 Check the results.

8. Ask a relative to write you a letter.

 When you receive the letter, hold it in your hand and tell what feelings come to you about what is inside the letter.

 Open the letter to check the results.

9. With one of your parents, look at photos of relatives they know but you do not know.

 Give your impressions about the people in the photos—
 * what they were like as children,
 * what they like to do,
 * what their names are, and so on.

10. Look at a picture of a famous historical person and give your impressions.
    - Where did he live?
    - What did he do?
    - What happened in his life?

    Go to the library or surf the Internet to check the results.

11. Have someone send you a picture on-line and see what impressions come to you.

    Check the results.

12. Before opening a present hold the present and see what you feel is inside.

    After all your impressions have been given open the present to check the results.

13. Visit a library, bookstore, or newsstand and hold a book or magazine without reading it.
    - Who are the characters in the book?
    - What is the story about?
    - Who is on the magazine cover?

    Give all the impressions that come to mind.

    Then open the book or magazine and check the results.

14. Choose three similar photos from a magazine: three children, three men smiling, three women smiling, three houses, three pets, and so on.

    Place each picture in an envelope and mix them up.

    Hold each separate envelope and give your impressions.

    After reading the last envelope open each envelope and compare the results.

15. Group Exercise: Everyone should write down his or her name on a separate piece of paper.

    Fold each piece of paper the same way, covering the name, and place all the pieces in a bag or a hat.

    Mix the folded papers well.

    Each child should pick a paper and hold it in his hand unopened and then say the name on the piece of paper.

    When everyone is done, check the results.

    Repeat the exercise as often as desired.

16. Group Exercise: Put twenty candies or objects of the same size but different colors—M&M's, PEZ, gummy bears, birthday candles—in a bag and mix them up.

    Have one child reach into the bag and hold the candy in his closed hand. Without looking, let each group member intuitively verbalize what color candy is in his hand.

    Choose another person to hold the candy, and repeat the exercise.

Aura Reading

All living things have colors. Our hair, eyes, and skin have color. A person's spirit and energy has color, too, called an Aura. Auras can be seen or sensed around all living things.

Every aura has three parts:

• The Physical Aura, which changes color daily as the body changes. The Physical Aura is closest to the body.

• The Mental/Emotional Aura, which changes color as a person's moods and emotions change during the day. The Mental/Emotional Aura is next to the Physical Aura.

• The Spiritual Aura, the color of a person's soul, changes least often.

There are no bad Auras or colors. Reading an Aura simply tells us about the person, animal, or plant. How they feel, what they want, what they need, and so on. Children, being visual, freely interpret such colors and information.

There is no best way to see an Aura. A child may see one part of it or several layers of colors at once. The colors may appear as emanating lines of color, a sense of color, or a block of color. It is best to let a child discover his own meaning for the color he sees or senses around a person. If there is confusion about these impressions, find a basic meaning for the color in the Aura Guide.

AURA GUIDE

Color	*Meaning*
Green	Growth, change
Yellow	New growth, beginnings
Blue	Balance, harmony, strength
Pink	Affection, kindness
Red	Anger, healing, love
Gray	Wisdom, quiet
Black	Independence, protection, isolation
Brown	Earthy, physical
White	Cleansing, clearing away
Purple	Unity, harmony, clarity
Orange	Serenity, peacefulness

AURA READING EXERCISES

1. To read your own Aura, face a mirror with a little light behind you.

   Stare at a place just a few inches above your shoulder or neck in the mirror.

   Let your eyes go out of focus.

   See if you can sense or see any color or colors rising from your shoulder or neck.

   Say what the colors make you feel or any other words that come to mind.

2. Look at your Aura in the morning in the same way as in the exercise above, and then look at it at night to see any differences.

3. Sit across from another person and place your hands a few inches from his shoulder or arm or chest and close your eyes.

   See if you can feel the person's Aura energy with your hands. What words come into your mind?

   Open your eyes and stare at the same spot on the person, letting your eyes go out of focus.
   - What colors do you see?
   - Are they the same?
   - What else comes to mind?

   Change places.

4. Now, with your eyes closed, stand or sit near another person, and extend your open hands a few inches from the other person's body to sense his aura.

   Relate any colors and intuitive information received during the Aura Reading.

5. Take a walk and find different natural objects: stones, driftwood, shells, sticks, leaves, grass.

Place them on the ground and read their Auras.

Place the objects, one at a time, in your open hand and read the Aura of each object.

Then read the Aura of your hand around the object, noticing any differences.

6. Sit with your parent or brother or sister in the morning and read each other's Aura.

Repeat this exercise several mornings and notice any differences.

7. Take a few natural foods—fruits, vegetables, nuts—and put them in a line a few inches from each other.

Look at each fruit or other food and read its Aura. Say any other words or thoughts that pop into your head about the fruit.

If you have never eaten the fruit, see if you can sense how it would taste based on your Aura Reading.

8. When you wake up in the morning, choose the color of your clothing based on how you are feeling.

Check in with yourself during the day and see how you feel about the colors you are wearing. Do they still suit your mood?

9. Find a box of crayons or colored pencils.

Close your eyes and sense the colors around your body or around the other people in the room.

Open your eyes and draw their bodies with their Auras around them.

See what other information comes into your head.

10. Draw pictures of your family, picking colors that you think describe each person.

    Before you show each family member your picture, ask him which color he "feels like" at that moment. Compare results.

11. Walk down the street, in a mall, or in a forest, and focus on letting your Aura grow like a light all around you, getting larger like a big bubble of color as you take each step. Notice how you feel. Do people walk into your Aura?

    Fill up all the spaces around you as far as you can. Do people walk around your Aura? Do animals come close to your Aura?

12. Group Exercise: Give everyone crayons or colored pencils. Pick one child to stand in front of everyone.

    Let everyone draw that person and his or her Aura.

    When everyone is finished, let each person describe the Aura he drew and add any other information that comes to him about it.

    Switch places until every group member has had his Aura drawn and read by others.

13. Group Exercise: Put two different objects in separate bags or boxes that look the same.

    Let everyone focus on one bag or box and read its Aura.

    Let each person say any impressions that come to mind about the object inside.

    Clear your minds and do the same with the other bag or box.

    When everyone is finished, open each box or bag and look at the object.

    Check the results. Use different objects and repeat.

Intuitive Healing

A kind touch, a warm hug, holding hands, and kissing are some natural healing ways in which children respond to people they love. Intuitive Healing focuses on sharing that loving energy to help people physically, mentally, emotionally, and spiritually heal themselves.

Intuitive Healing is the oldest form of healing known to humanity. It is a simple process of laying on of hands to transfer loving energy into the body of another person so that the person can use the energy to heal himself. In addition, intuitive insights are given during the Intuitive Healing to help the person restore his mental, physical, emotional, and spiritual balance.

Although Intuitive Healing is not a replacement for any medical doctor or practitioner, it is a positive addition to a person's own healing process. The person being healed may always choose to accept or reject the loving energy and insights offered to him by the Intuitive Healer.

INTUITIVE HEALING EXERCISES

1. Practice Releasing Tension.
   Then place the palm of one open hand right in front of your forehead (where your eyebrows meet) without touching your face. Close your eyes and see if you can sense the energy coming from your hand.
   - Can you feel it?
   - Is it pushing energy toward your face?
   - Or taking it away?

   Shake out your hand and place your other hand in front of your forehead in the same way.
   - Is it pushing energy toward your face?

- Or taking it away?
- Are both hands doing the same thing or is each doing something different?

Try this exercise at different times of the day and notice any differences.

2. Try exercise number 1 with another person.

Sit across from each other and repeat the steps for the exercise, holding your hand in front of the other's forehead.

Talk about your results.

3. Take two inexpensive plants or start two plants from seed.

Place them in two same-size pots, each with the same amount of soil.

Water each the same way.

Choose one plant to receive healing energy.

Every day do Intuitive Healing only on that one plant, first practicing Releasing Tension, then placing a hand or both hands on or around the plant or pot and sending healing energy to the plant for as long as you like. Do this as many times as you wish.

Notice if there is any difference in the growth of the two plants over time.

4. Try exercise number 3 on a family member or pet, sending your loving energy to that person or animal.

5. Practice Releasing Tension.

Place your hands on another person's shoulders and focus on sending the energy from your hands through his shoulders down to his feet.

Let the other person tell you what he is feeling inside his body.

Reverse positions.

6. With a friend or family member, stand or sit a short distance from each other. Practice Releasing Tension.

Let one person place a hand or hands in front of the other's face (without touching it) and send energy through his hands to warm the other person's face.

Say what each of you is feeling during the exercise.

Switch positions and begin again.

7. If a parent or someone you love is away or lives far away, call that person on the telephone.

Then practice Releasing Tension and, placing both hands on the receiver, send healing energy to him through your hands and the receiver.

Let him tell you what he feels.

Try this at different times of the day and on different days to notice any differences.

8. With another person, practice Releasing Tension.

Then place your hands on or near the other person's forehead.

Focus on sending your healing energy to a part of his body—his feet, his left knee, his shoulder—but do not tell the person where you are sending the healing energy.

Let the other person tell you where in his body he is feeling the healing energy.

Try to send healing energy to other places in his body. If you wish, clear your mind and shake out your hands before you try again.

Reverse positions.

9. If a family member is away or sick, or a pet is at the vet-
   erinarian's, practice Releasing Tension.
   Send healing energy to him.
   Focus on him or on a photo of him.
   Place your hands on the photo or just extend them and
   let your healing energy be sent through your hands
   into the photo or the air to your pet or relative.
   This exercise can be done as many times as you wish.
   Check for results.

10. Find several crystals.
    Practice Releasing Tension and then place one crystal in
    your open hand. Close your eyes and see if you can
    sense any healing energy from the crystal.
    Choose another crystal and repeat the exercise until you
    have sensed the healing energy in each crystal.
    Notice any differences.
    If you find a crystal with healing energy, hold it in your
    hand while you practice any of the other Intuitive
    Healing exercises. Its healing energy will be added to
    yours.

11. Group Exercise: Healing Circle.
    Practice Releasing Tension and then join hands and form
    a circle.
    Focus on sending healing energy through your hands so
    that everyone in the circle is sending healing energy.
    Let the energy build. If anyone feels uncomfortable and
    wishes to leave the Healing Circle he can; but the peo-
    ple on either side of him should make sure to join hands
    as he steps away so the healing energy can continue.

Proceed until most of the people in the circle wish to stop.

12. Group Exercise: Personal Healing Circle.
Follow the instructions for a Healing Circle but choose one person to sit or stand in the center of the circle.
All the members in the circle can either join hands and focus sending healing energy to the person in the center or can hold their open hands facing the person and send healing energy to him.
The person in the center of the circle should tell what he is feeling. He can stop the healing at any time.
This can also be done long-distance by placing the name or a photograph of the person or persons you wish to send healing energy to in the center of the circle.

Clairvoyance

Clairvoyance is the ability to see or sense situations, people, or objects in visions or symbols. It is the most visual form of psychic ability. Everyone uses their natural clairvoyant talents when they dream. A clairvoyant is able to see such things while awake and can give impressions about the past and present and make predictions.

Clairvoyance is naturally experienced when we receive intuitive dreams, talk to imaginary playmates, see or sense colors or soul lights, and visualize situations before they occur. Many cherished games passed from generation to generation include Clairvoyance as a necessary part. See if you recognize some of them.

CLAIRVOYANCE EXERCISES

1. Clear your mind. Using the inside of your forehead or a blank wall, focus on a parent, an older family member, or a friend's parent and get a picture in your mind of what that person looked like as a child.

   Describe everything you see or any other thoughts that come to your mind.

   Then look at a photograph of that person as a child to check your results.

2. Clear your mind. Using the inside of your forehead or a blank wall to focus upon, ask another person to choose a category—
   - favorite color
   - food
   - their last vacation
   - a job
   - favorite basketball player
   - singer

   —and see if you can visualize that in your mind.

   Tell everything you see and any thoughts that pop into your mind.

3. Clear your mind and have someone flip a coin in the air.
   Before the coin reaches the floor visualize if the coin will land heads or tails.
   Do this ten times.

4. Clear your mind while someone puts four different-colored balls, crayons, or balls of paper into a closed container, laying them from left to right.
   Visualize the order of the objects by their colors.
   Check your results.

Repeat, with the order of the objects changed each time.

5. Cut three pictures of men or women or objects out of a magazine or newspaper.

Look closely at the pictures and then go into another room.

Have another person place the pictures face up, lining them from left to right.

From the other room describe each picture in order.

Check the results.

Repeat, with the order of the pictures changed.

6. Have a person fill a cup with water and place his hands around the cup while he thinks of a question, then asks it.

When he is done have him place the cup in front of you.

Clear your mind, then stare into the water, letting your eyes go unfocused.

Do not touch the cup. If you do not wish to stare into the water, close your eyes and focus on the inside of your forehead. Do whatever is comfortable for you.

See what impressions and pictures come to mind and verbalize them.

If you have trouble seeing anything, let the other person ask another question, and repeat.

7. Put twenty different-colored marbles, colored candies of the same shape, or crumpled pieces of colored paper in a bag or box.

Mix up the contents.

Close your eyes and reach into the bag or box and take one object and hold it in your hand.

See if you can visualize the color of the object.

Open your eyes and hand and see the results.
Repeat the exercise.

8. Lay ten playing cards facedown on a table.
   Clear your mind and focus on the first card. See if it is
      red or black.
   Then see what number or picture is on the card.
   Turn the card over and check your results.
   Continue until all the cards are turned over.
   Then repeat the exercise using ten other cards until all
      the cards are read.

9. Take two different-colored pieces of paper, candies, or
      other objects that will fit inside your closed hand and
      show them to a partner.
   Place your hands behind your back and close your hands
      around each object.
   Have your partner clear his mind and visualize which ob-
      ject is in your right hand and which is in your left hand.
   Check the results.
   Repeat this exercise, changing candies each time.
   You can also do this exercise with just one object, leav-
      ing one hand empty. Your partner can visualize which
      hand holds the candy.

10. When you get up in the morning, clear your mind and
      then visualize what your friends will be wearing to
      school that day.
    Check the results when you get to school.

11. Place three small items under three cups of the same de-
       sign and size. Make sure the cups cover the items
       completely.

Close your eyes and have a partner move the cups around and place them in a line.

When he says "ready," visualize which item is under each cup.

Lift each cup to check the results.

Repeat the exercise several times.

12. Group Exercise: Choose one person to sit in the next room or out of sight of the others. When everyone has cleared their minds and closed their eyes have someone say "ready."

The person in the other room should do something physical like shaking his right hand, covering his eyes, or moving his leg.

Have him come back into the room and let each member of the group tell the person what he saw him doing.

Check the results and switch places until everyone has had a chance.

13. Group Exercise: Place five different-shaped objects on a tray or board.

Show them to the others and then remove the objects from sight.

Rearrange the objects from left to right.

Say "ready" when finished, and return to the room.

Everyone clears their minds and focuses on the objects from left to right.

When everyone is finished, bring the objects in and check the results. Repeat the exercise.

14. Group Exercise: Close your eyes while the others find hiding places. Count to ten and then clear your mind.

Visualize where each person is and find them.

When everyone is found, switch places.

OR Close your eyes and have one person hide an object in the room.

When the object is hidden, clear your mind and visualize where the object is hidden.

As you move, the others can tell you if you are getting "warm" (closer) or "cold" (farther away from it). Keep visualizing until you reach it.

Switch places.

15. Group Exercise: You will need a button that can fit inside your hand.

   Form a circle and choose one person to go out of the room.

   Pick one person in the circle to hold the button, and then have everyone put their closed hands behind their backs. Let the person come back into the room.

   Standing in the center of the circle, he should close his eyes and visualize who is holding the button.

   He then steps in front of that person, who shows him his hands.

   Repeat the exercise.

16. Group Exercise: Put a jar or container in a classroom or a room in your home.

   Throughout the week, take a moment to clear your mind and then visualize any future situations or predictions for your school, your family, or your town or city. Write down your predictions, with the date, and put them in the jar.

   At the end of the week, read to see which predictions came true.

   Repeat the exercise every week.

17. Group Exercise: Draw a picture of an animal—without its tail—and place it on a wall. Cut out a tail for the

animal from a separate piece of heavy paper. Place a piece of tape on the back of the tail so it will stick to the picture of the animal.

With your eyes closed or blindfolded, turn in circles several times and then have someone point you in the direction of the picture.

Holding the tail in your hand, clear your mind and visualize where the tail should be.

Move toward that place and stick the tail to the picture.

Open your eyes and check results.

Switch places until everyone has a chance to play.

OR Fill a bag with candies and hang it within reach from a post or the ceiling.

Take a rubber or plastic bat and, with your eyes closed or blindfolded, turn around three times, clear your mind, visualize where the bag is, and swing the bat three times at the bag to open it.

Check the results and switch places.

18. Group Exercise: Stand inside a circle and close your eyes while everyone in the circle joins hands and moves around you.

When you are ready, say stop. Everyone stops moving.

Clear your mind and visualize the person standing in front of you; say his name out loud.

Open your eyes and check the results.

Repeat the exercise and switch places.

Psychokinesis and Levitation

Bend objects with your bare hands. Leap tall buildings in a single bound.

You don't have to be Superman to accomplish such feats. You simply have to use psychokinetic ability.

Psychokinesis is the ability to move or change physical matter using spiritual energy. Bending a spoon, moving a physical object, and stopping the hands of a clock or other machinery without using physical force are ways of demonstrating Psychokinesis.

Levitation, lifting objects without using physical power, is thought by some scholars to have been a way in which the ancient pyramids in Egypt and Central America were built. Psychokinesis and Levitation are being examined and tested in both the United States and the former Soviet Union today for their possible benefits to modern society.

PSYCHOKINESIS EXERCISES

1. Take a feather and place it in a large bowl or dish of water. Clear your mind and with your eyes open or closed visualize moving the feather from left to right. Check the results without touching the bowl.

2. There are three ways to bend a metal object. Take a key, spoon, or fork and:

   Visualize a bright ball of light around your head and bring that light into your arms and hands and fingers. Let the ball of light grow bright in your hands and then place both hands on the metal object, sending the ball of light into the point where you want the object to bend.

Continue sending the light and see if the object bends.

Practice Releasing Tension and then decide what part of the object you wish to bend.

Close your eyes and try to see the bent object in your mind.

Keeping that image in your mind, hold the object in your hand or hands and send white light into your arms and hands and fingers, like a laser beam, to the spot where you want the object to bend.

You may also send white light energy from the point between your eyebrows to the spot on the object.

Do this for as long as you wish.

Practice Releasing Tension and visualize a spot on the object where you want it to bend.

Rub the selected spot on the object very fast with your hands or fingers.

When you are finished, practice Releasing Tension and then leave the object alone for a short while.

Check the results.

3. Tie a feather or penny to a string and let it dangle from a table or counter.

Sit before the feather and bring in white light energy as in exercise number 2 and either put your hands before the feather or use your white light from your forehead to see if you can move the feather. Make sure you do not breathe on the feather and that your hands do not touch the feather while you do the exercise.

4. Take two ice cubes of the same size and place each in a glass on a table or the floor in front of you.

Using the same routine as in exercise 2, focus on melting

one ice cube. Check to see if that ice cube melted more quickly.

5. Set three boxes beside one another on a floor or other flat surface.

   Hold a feather a few feet above the boxes.

   Just as you release the feather send white light energy to the feather and visualize the feather falling into your chosen box.

   Check the results and repeat.

6. Tie a button or other small object to a string, attach the string to the end of a table, and let it dangle. Steady the object so it does not move.

   Try to visualize moving the button or object in one direction—forward, backward, clockwise, counter-clockwise—using your white light energy from your hands or from the center of your forehead without touching the object.

   Practice Releasing Tension and try again.

7. Toss a coin.

   While the coin is in the air, focus on making it land on heads and visualize it.

   Check the results.

   Try the exercise again, focusing on the coin landing on tails.

8. Find books and information at a library or bookstore or on the Internet about how to build your own miniature pyramid.

   Follow the directions and build a small pyramid out of wood or cardboard.

Then place a blunt-pointed pencil, piece of hard cheese, crystal, or other object in the very center of the pyramid and leave it there for several days.

Check results daily, noting any changes in the object.

9. Group Exercise: Choose one person to leave the room so that he cannot hear the others.

Have the group decide which direction they want to move him—left, right, forward, or backward.

When the direction has been chosen and the person returns, have him stand in front of everyone.

Practice Releasing Tension and have them begin to send white light energy through their hands or from between their eyebrows toward the person, visualizing the chosen direction.

The person can either verbalize his feelings or move in that direction.

Repeat the exercise with another person.

10. Group Exercise: Send one person out of the room.

Form a circle and choose one group member to focus upon. When the person returns, have him stand in the middle of the circle facing the others.

Give him a rubber stick to use as a pointer.

While the others in the circle visualize moving the pointer toward the chosen person, let the person in the center slowly move until his stick is pointing at the group member where he feels he should stop.

Check results and then repeat with others.

LEVITATION EXERCISE

Before lifting a heavy object or riding a bicycle up a steep hill, place your hands, palms down, a few inches above the object or bicycle so that one hand is directly above the other and both are above the bicycle or object.

Allow white light energy to build from your hands above the bicycle or object.

Then slowly remove each hand and see if lifting the object or pedaling the bicycle up the hill is any easier.

Mediumship

Mediumship is the ability to sense and channel nonphysical or soul energy. Very sensitive children can feel other people's emotions, and respond to the nonphysical energies of people and natural things.

A medium or channeler of this energy can receive messages from loved ones, gain impressions about physical events and people that relate to the past, present, or future, and sense the presence of angels, imaginary playmates, or spirit guides.

MEDIUMISTIC EXERCISES

1. Take a small object and tie it to a string. Place the other end of the string between two of your fingers and let the object dangle in front of you.

   Decide on a movement of the object—back and forth, circular, and so on—that means "yes" and one that means "no."

   Then holding the object from the string very still ask a yes-or-no question and notice the object's movements.

   Continue with other questions.

   Check the results.

2. Place a closed container of food in front of someone so that he cannot see or smell it.

   Practice Releasing Tension and see if the other person can

identify the contents.
Then open the container and taste the food.
Switch foods and places.

3. Take a walk and stop near flowers, trees, animals, and
    other natural things, without studying them.
    With your eyes closed or open sense each natural thing,
    and say any words or impressions that come to mind.
    Then focus your sight on the object and describe what
    you see.
    Repeat.

4. Draw or tell a story about an invisible playmate or angel.

5. Without looking at a CD or tape, see if you can sense the
    type of music
    • and the instruments
    • the name of the person or group
    • title of CD
    Change CDs and repeat.

6. Draw a picture or tell a story about things or people you
    see in your dreams.

7. Focus on a friend or family member. See if you can sense
    • what he will be eating for dinner,
    • what he will be doing during the summer,
    • what presents he will receive on his birthday, and so
      on.
    Check the results.

8. Group Exercise: Sit facing a partner and place your open palms in front of your partner's head or face, then close your eyes.

   Sense what he is feeling and any other information that comes into your mind and say it.

   Open your eyes and look at your partner, touch him, talk to him. Notice the differences between what you sensed and felt.

   Repeat with other partners.

Telepathy

Using Telepathy is like being a human telephone. It is the ability to know or send a thought, idea, image, or impression from the mind of one person to that of another. From birth, everyone naturally uses telepathic talents for communication. Telepathy is the most physically oriented of all intuitive abilities. Through Intuitive Reading we can gain information about a person's past, present, and future, but when we use Telepathy we focus only on information in the moment, sent from one person's mind to another's.

There are two basic parts in Telepathy: sending the information and receiving the information. Someone may be a strong Sender. Another may be a better Receiver. Some will find that they are equally good at sending *and* receiving telepathic information.

It is important to note that Telepathy is not mind control. If at any time a person does not wish to or is unable to receive or send impressions, nothing will happen. When a person does receive telepathic impressions from a Sender, he does not have to act on them unless he wishes to do so.

TELEPATHY EXERCISES

1. While a baby crawls around a room, focus on sending a simple thought or word directing him where you want him to go. See what happens.

2. With a partner, decide who will be the Sender and who will be the Receiver.
   Clear your minds and have the Sender think of something inside the room, backyard, or play area.
   Send that image, or words describing it, to the Receiver.
   Receiver, say anything that pops into your mind either in words or pictures.
   If you have difficulty, practice Releasing Tension or ask a few questions to narrow your choices.
   Change places.

3. With a partner, decide who will be the Sender and who will be the Receiver. Then decide on a category—animals, people, flowers, television shows, and so on.
   Both Sender and Receiver take a pencil or crayons and a piece of paper and move out of each other's sight.
   When you both have cleared your minds, Sender, draw your chosen item from the category while sending each part of what you are drawing in words or pictures in your mind to the Receiver.
   Receiver, as you get information, draw it on your piece of paper.
   Check the results.
   Sender and Receiver exchange places and categories to begin again.

4. With a partner—one Sender, one Receiver—place four different circles of colors on a piece of blank paper

between you. Sender, choose one color and mentally
    send it in picture or words to the Receiver.
Receiver, when you receive the color you must point to
    the circle of color you received.
Change places or add colors and repeat.

5. Sender, take a deck of playing cards. When ready choose
    a card at random, look at it out of view of the Receiver,
    and begin sending the picture or words describing the
    card to him.
    Receiver, verbalize all your impressions.
    Check the results.
    Repeat using other cards and then switch places.
    You can also do this exercise sending impressions on the
    color of the card only.

6. If a pet or animal is nearby, call the pet to you, saying his
    name silently in your mind, and see if your pet re-
    sponds.
    Try this several times during the day.

7. Choose a state, state capital, country, famous historical
    figure, or the like and send an image or thought about
    it to a Receiver.
    Receiver, verbalize all your impressions.
    Change places and categories as desired.

8. Choose a Sender and Receiver.
    Sender, think of a number from one to ten and send it to
    the Receiver in a word or number.
    Receiver, when the number is received verbalize it.
    Check results.
    Both clear your minds.

Repeat the exercise using any number from one to fifty, then one to one hundred.

Check results and switch places.

9. Choose a Sender; Sender, send a physical sensation—hot, cold, soft, hard, and so on to a Receiver in a mental word, feeling, or picture.

Receiver, when you have obtained the information, verbalize it or act it out.

Switch places.

10. Choose a day and have a Sender call a Receiver's name in sound or letters in your mind several times during the day. Make note of the times when the name is sent.

Receiver, upon receiving your name, write down the times when it is received.

Check your results.

Switch days and places.

11. Before answering the telephone, focus on receiving the name or image of the person who is calling.

Answer the phone and check your results.

12. Sender, choose five different objects, colors, or people.

At a time agreed upon by both Sender and Receiver, Sender, send each object separately to the Receiver, who is situated some distance away.

Check the results.

13. Group Exercise: Choose one person to be the Sender and have him stand in the front of a group of Receivers.

When the Sender is ready, send the image or word of "right" hand or "left" hand.

As each Receiver receives the impression, lift that hand.

When all Receivers have finished, check results.

Repeat this exercise using fingers or legs.

Switch Senders.

OR Have each Receiver use a pencil and paper.

Sender focuses on sending the image or word of a body part—nose, ear, face, and so on.

When the Receivers receive the information, write down the images.

When all information has been received, check the results.

Switch Senders.

14. Group Exercise: Choose a Sender and have him hide an object in another room out of sight of the Receivers.

Sender, when ready, mentally send the image or words telling where the object is located and have Receivers find the object telepathically. The Receiver who finds it becomes the next Sender.

Repeat the exercise.

15. Group Exercise: Choose three Senders.

Senders form a line in front of the group as numbers, one, two, and three.

All Receivers turn away while Senders change places.

When ready, each Sender, in turn, sends his number to the Receivers. When all information is received, Receivers turn and face Senders to check results.

Repeat, using three other Senders.

16. Group Exercise: Divide a group in half, into Senders and Receivers.

With Receivers' backs turned, Senders decide on a number to send, from one to ten.

When everyone is ready, Senders send the chosen number to Receivers.

Receivers say the number as they receive it.

Check the results. Then switch Senders and Receivers.

Repeat the exercise, using numbers from one to one hundred, colors, countries, historical figures, and so on.

17. Group Exercise: Choose one Sender. Decide on five different commands: a baby step, a huge step, two hopping steps, and so on.

All Receivers form a line standing several feet from the Sender and all facing the Sender.

As the Sender calls the name of a Receiver, he sends a telepathic command to that Receiver.

When the Receiver receives the command he takes whatever step he visualizes. If the Receiver is right he remains in place, having moved closer to the Sender. If he is wrong, he goes back to his original position.

Each Receiver gets a turn until one Receiver reaches the Sender and touches him. That person becomes the next Sender and all begin again.

Common Questions and Answers

Are girls more intuitively talented than boys?

In modern Western society, girls tend to score higher than boys do on tests that measure intuitive ability. This result is based somewhat more on cultural and social differences than on individual abilities. Since all children have intuitive abilities, the degree to which the abilities are used, and how comfortable children are with them, are often determined by the environment in which they are living. In an open atmosphere both boys and girls, as individuals, can develop and acknowledge and use their very special talents freely.

Will relying on Feeling Response encourage a child to be selfish and not to think of others?

Acknowledging a Feeling Response does quite the opposite. It encourages children to know their feelings about any situation in an honest, holistic way and also to respect the rights of others to know their feelings even when their feelings differ. Rather than base reactions and decisions on monetary desires, jealousy, or the thoughts of others, children using Feeling Response as a natural part of themselves begin to acknowledge and understand what they are feeling and to recognize that others have the right to make their own decisions.

Can children release too much energy during Releasing Tension exercises?

Releasing Tension exercises do not deplete children's energy. They simply help children to let go of pent-up energies that have been accumulated during the day and that are no longer needed to maintain their energy balance. Though the body releases these energies very naturally, Releasing Tension exercises allow the body to release them all at once.

Will teaching children about different types of intuitive abilities confuse them? Should they be taught these abilities in some sort of order or one at a time?

There is no prescribed order in which to teach intuitive abilities. One such ability is no greater or less than another, and all children already have their intuitive abilities within. Learning about the different types of these natural abilities will encourage them to experiment and to discover their talents fully. Many children will be interested in trying various exercises for different types of abilities and will combine several different exercises rather than follow them in a regimented way. In the end, their natural interests and spontaneity will lead them toward those talents that are uniquely theirs.

Can developing intuitive abilities be dangerous to children? Do children need to be a certain age to develop and use these abilities?

Children's intuitive abilities are already used in very natural ways during their day. Spontaneous impressions voiced for no reason, telepathic information, vivid dreams—all this can be better understood by developing their innate abilities. Children are often more balanced than adults in determining what they can or cannot do when developing their intuitive talents. If an exercise is too difficult, they will avoid it or show a lack of interest. If children cannot verbalize their impressions but are interested in exploring some exercises, the exercises can be varied to suit their skills or means of expression. Allow them to participate in creating their own exercises. It is more harmful to teach children to fear or ignore a natural part of themselves than to let them explore all the parts of themselves, especially those that can be positive tools for their own development.

What if children do not get tangible results from the exercises?

The goal is not to achieve perfect results but to acquaint children with their own talents. Children will have accurate results in some exercises and not in others, even in areas where they show pronounced talent. This may be due to their inability to focus at the time, a need for approval, or pressure to perform. They may try the same exercise or a variation later and get results. With practice, they will become more accustomed to using their intuitive abilities and developing them. A focus on the process, not so much on the results, will enable children to explore their potential with comfort and freedom.

What if the children are too young to speak? How can you work with them to develop their intuitive abilities?

Working with exercises that use Telepathy or encouraging them to draw or dance or act out their impressions will help them to practice their intuitive abilities and later to incorporate these abilities with their verbal development.

Thirteen-year-old Ravi never handed in homework and had a hard time retaining information. Tested in school, he was diagnosed as being borderline retarded and put in special classes. In the spring, a substitute teacher named Karin assigned Ravi some special schoolwork: to write a poem about love. For the first time in years Ravi handed in homework. The poetry he had written was maturely composed and went far beyond the mental potential indicated by the psychologists.

"Please Mommy. Let me play piano," Alessandra begged at age three. Although no one in the family was musically inclined, her mother finally took her to a piano teacher. At age five she was able to play Mozart concertos and began composing her own classical music. At age six she started winning state musical competitions. By age ten Alessandra performed as a solo artist with the San Francisco philharmonic orchestra.

At fifteen Samuel was known for his mature wisdom. His peers would come to him for advice and direction. He was seldom wrong. One day Samuel advised a classmate not to go to the pizza parlor at four o'clock to meet his friend. Laughing at Samuel's advice, the classmate went anyway. A few minutes after four o'clock, a person ran into the restaurant with a gun and shot the cashier and robbed the register, injuring one other person—Samuel's classmate.

5

Nurturing the Sixth Sense in Children

Intuitively gifted children may consistently read people like a book. They may see things that are invisible to others. They may naturally sense and converse with spirit guides, angels, or loved ones who have passed on. They may forecast future events without thinking and achieve goals far beyond their chronological age.

Such children, extraordinarily gifted, are still emotionally, physically, and psychologically unformed. They cannot understand why everyone does not feel what they feel. Why they are ridiculed when they know they are right. Why people don't express themselves when they obviously know what they are feeling.

Intuitively Gifted Children

In primitive cultures, children with exceptional intuitive talents were treated as special godly gifts bestowed upon their people. Elders listened to them. They were respected and carefully nurtured in the ways of the shamans and holy people that came before them. Other children looked up to them as special role models. There was no doubt among their people that they would become leaders, healers, matriarchs and patriarchs of their group. No one thought them odd. No one ignored their invisible talents. No one ostracized them.

The opposite is true in Western society. In medieval times intuitively gifted children were feared, damned, thrown in dungeons, or hanged. Under the Inquisition, children demonstrating supernatural visions or powers were tortured, hanged, or burned at the stake. In colonial times in North America, children who were even thought to have intuitive dreams or perceptions that could not be physically proven were ostracized, ridiculed, and punished before the whole community. In 1692, in Salem, Massachusetts, whole segments of the young population, especially females, were accused of witchcraft and heresy if they as much as mentioned anything intuitively derived. People feared for their lives and families if their children could be accused of having intuitive powers.

In modern Western societies, children with these same talents may not be killed but are still feared, ridiculed, or ostracized. Children with exceptional sixth sense abilities are looked upon as weird, crazy, learning impaired, or dangerously different from their peers.

Highly intuitive children are neither odd nor psychologically impaired. They are talented. Their intuitive talents are so pronounced they cannot dismiss them. Strong psychological defenses cannot block them from using those talents. Misunderstood, they go through life believing all their wonderful "invisible" talents hinder them from being accepted, worthy, bright, and capable.

"Just go to your room," ten-year-old Jeffrey's mother commanded.

"Why?" he asked.

"Because I said so. That's why," she responded with anger.

"But you're not mad at me. You're mad because Dad's not home yet."

His mother looked at him and became livid. "Just go to your room! Now!" She had no defense as she watched her angered son run up the stairs.

She knew he was right.

Intuitively gifted children are unusual in their emotional sensitivities. They know why people are upset. They sense people's moods without being told. They understand events without witnessing them. Without conscious knowledge of their perceptions they become confused. When a teacher picks on them, they become upset knowing that the teacher is just having a bad day. They do not understand why friends are not kind and are dishonest about their own inner insecurities. They are humiliated when family members laugh at their observations. They become flustered when parents refuse to show their feelings. They are uncomfortable when their strong insights are ignored.

Intuitively gifted children are usually well integrated. They are also intellectually bright and creative beyond their chronological years. Because they see things through the eyes of an old soul they are commonly treated as adults by adults throughout their childhood. They are usually given more emotional responsibility than others their age and are consistently expected to do or be more than they are physically capable of doing or being. They live in a world of daily conflict between trying to live up to adult expectations and being accepted by their peers. Along the way they suffer for their psychological and emotional differences.

Adults often rely on intuitively gifted children's insights, putting an even greater sense of emotional responsibility on their very young shoulders. Place three teenage boys together and the one who does not fit in—who often acts like an adult, an outsider—is probably an intuitively gifted child. He may sacrifice his natural talents to try to fit into any group. He may suffer in school because he must be all things to all people and often feels emotionally drained, depressed, withdrawn, or repressed due to his acute awareness of and sensitivity to everything around him. The inability of adults and peers to understand the dilemma of being an old soul in a young body leaves these children at odds with themselves.

In school, intuitively gifted children find themselves in another unspoken dilemma in which they may be unable to voice their deep feelings and fears because no one will understand them. They may react to teachers' moods. They may be distracted by classmates' activities yet torn between the teachers' frustration and their own inherent need to fit in. They may have difficulty memorizing facts and terms that have no conceptual meaning for them. Explain Einstein's process in discovering the theory of relativity and they will remember it. Describe the social climate of the time Lincoln freed the slaves and they will not forget the date. Their way of learning through perspective, conceptualization, wisdom, and vision directly conflicts with classroom methods based on rating intelligence by multiple-choice exams.

These children may be exceptionally bright and uncommonly creative, but their inner talents are ignored in traditionally structured learning settings because their perceptions and ways of achieving results do not fit in. Such highly gifted children often feel like failures and losers, developing low self-esteem and depression in the classroom and at home. Outwardly they may appear lazy or reticent, or they may even use their pronounced intuitive abilities manipulatively to get by or to gain negative reinforcement.

Intuitively attuned children often use their sixth sense to read their teachers or parents—to charm them or act out behaviorally to avoid their demands. They know just how far to push a parent to get what they want and when to stop. They know when people's intentions are sincere. They may be so withdrawn they cannot participate in any activity, or need to control their environment so that they do not feel so out of balance. They become problem children. They are the first to initiate negative situations with insincere teachers and also the first to stop others from distracting the well-intentioned ones. They may be the "good" girls or boys who work well below their capabilities. Or they may fight or be overactive when dishonest displays of emotion, caring, or discipline are shown.

Regardless of their outward behavior, intuitively gifted children are deeply aware of when they disappoint families, teachers, and friends. They are pained by their real feelings, and by their inability to produce desired grades, conform to specified behavior, or give or gain respect. Building inner pressures cause them to make foolish choices and behave contrary to the deeper feelings they cannot understand. They agonize over the opinions of family members who consistently misunderstand them. They suffer when teachers misinterpret their reactions to things they cannot consciously control. They are uncomfortable with friends who do not accept their often mature insights. Not understanding the reasons for their differences, these highly talented children suffer in silence. They remain isolated or lonely, suspecting that no one else knows or can relate to what they are feeling. They start to believe that there really is something very wrong with them and dread social situations, fearing disappointment in themselves and from others. Some actually become so depressed and helpless they try to physically hurt or destroy themselves.

In the past twenty years, in schools and communities all over the world, programs have been designed to fit the needs and talents of intellectually gifted children, athletically gifted children, and creatively gifted children. To date there are no programs that study or acknowledge intuitively gifted children.

This does not mean that every school must have a separate psychic class teaching children how to read auras, read minds, and so on. Intuitive abilities are not necessarily exclusive of any other talents. Children, in fact, naturally combine their intuitive talents with many other abilities. Intellectually gifted children use their intuition to understand and solve mentally difficult problems. Athletically gifted children have an intuitive sense of timing and an ability to find the elusive "zone" in sports. Creatively gifted children add their unseen vision and inspiration to their artistic talents. Like all gifted children, intuitively gifted children need to have their unique talents acknowledged and recognized. Then they can be proud of themselves and thrive in a society that accepts multidimensional people.

> *"Tommy just figured out how to start this old radio I've been tinkering with for the last three years."*
>
> *"Yvette knows how to style hair better than I can even imagine."*
>
> *"When I take Felicia to a museum she knows more about dinosaurs than the curator."*

When parents, teachers, and other adults recognize and nurture these gifted children's natural sixth sense, they encourage them to build self-esteem and self-reliance without injecting fear and feelings of isolation. Highly sensitive, intuitively gifted children need honest reinforcement that tells them there are positive and tangible uses for their unseen talents in everyday life. They need to feel support and respect from the people close to them; they need to know that their natural abilities are special.

Listening to them without editing their feelings or thoughts, allowing them to trust their intuition, and letting them see when they are right without judgment will help them to believe in themselves, rely on themselves, and use their talents to remain healthy and vital to benefit others.

There are many ways a parent, teacher, or friend can consciously help intuitively gifted children feel comfortable with their special talents:

• Do not push them to perform. No matter how astounding their abilities may seem, they are not entertainment. Being naturally empathetic and highly attuned to the needs of others, intuitively gifted children want to do things to please those they love. Usually precocious, at an early age they learn quickly that performing "on command" will assure love and acceptance. They may begin to see their talents as a way to gain approval rather than as tools for their own development. When they do not produce tangible desired effects using their intuitive abilities, they feel like failures and are less able to appreciate what they can do. But with positive reinforcement instead, such children can develop their abilities and become a sensitive teacher, a noted researcher, a talented doctor, a successful lawyer, a creative artist, or an insightful therapist rather than a carnival act.

• Do not force children to explore or develop their sixth sense in a structured way if they do not wish to do so. Since children view their talents as a natural part of themselves, they may not want or be able to separate them from their normal way of being. Since intuitively gifted children are quite sensitive, forcing them may inhibit them more. Listen to them. Make up mutual games where no one has to pass or fail. No matter how obvious their talent, it is best to help children find their own way rather than force them to do so.

• Create a receptive atmosphere in which children are free to observe the results of using their intuition and they will feel more inclined to experience and discuss it. Gentle guidance and encouragement will help children to recognize and fully develop these talents without making them feel that their every move is being studied.

• Do not focus on using the wisdom, advice, and insights of intuitively gifted children for your personal ends. Such children may be more than able to find right answers, solve adult problems, and give valuable information to help you in your life. But making them your personal gurus inhibits the use of their natural talents in their own personal growth. Open yourself to the possibility of discovering your own intuitive talents along with them. An atmosphere open to experimentation and fun can enable intuitively gifted children to connect with others while exploring their own individuality.

• Intuitively gifted children are often extremely talented individuals with many other assets to develop. To force competition or to focus exclusively on or ignore their intuitive abilities does not help them develop into well-rounded people. Cultivating the special talents that appear in the course of everyday life helps them integrate those talents and reach their full potential.

• Keep communication open about anything, no matter how silly it seems. Though wise beyond their physical years, intuitively gifted children are not adults. They are still undeveloped emotionally and physically. They need help in developing their physical knowledge, logic, dexterity, and expression of physical emotions, along with discovering their intuitive talents.

• Encourage independence. Whether exploring their sixth sense or any other talent, give children room to explore things in their own way without needless expectations or rules. Encouraging children to rely on their knowing and intuition allows them to feel good about themselves and take steps in trusting what they innately know.

• Find adult role models who also integrate their talents. Exposing children to viable, responsible, loving adults who are also intuitively gifted helps them gain more knowledge about and respect for their own talents. The role models need not be psychics or people who work in the intuitive field. If a child is athletically inclined, find a coach, trainer, or instructor who can help him discover his intuitive sense of timing to complement his athletic abilities. Since most coaches and trainers do not openly profess to using intuitive talents, use your gut reaction or Feeling Response when selecting an instructor.

• Encourage creative activities. Intuitively gifted children are creative in their thinking and organizational skills, and many manifest their creativity through art, music, dance, writing, drama, science, or social interaction. Allow time for them to investigate these talents and talk about their discoveries afterward.

• After finding adequate tutors or teachers, educate them about the specific problems of intuitively gifted children so that they can clearly understand their special talents and needs and find better ways to help them learn. Incorporating their invisible talents into the learning process can further their intellectual and social education and help these children flourish in the classroom.

• Allow children to create special projects at home and in school. Give them the freedom to develop these projects in their own way with gentle guidance. In this way, intuitively talented children can learn how to use their natural talents in socially structured situations.

• Create an atmosphere where intuitively gifted children can openly question things they do not understand without being made to feel strange or stupid. If you cannot answer a question, do not dismiss the question or make up an answer. Intuitive children sense when you are lying. Encourage them to explore possibilities and seek out more information about a given subject or idea. It will strengthen the loving bond between you.

• Do not limit intuitive children in their learning about things. Let their driving interest be their guide. If they want to pursue a project or idea that may seem too mature for them or is not included in their classroom curriculum, give them room to explore it. They will reach their own natural limit of understanding and go on to other activities. Many adults are afraid to allow children to trust their intuition or try something that might seem too difficult for them. Intuitively gifted children, in touch with their gut reactions, will know what feels right for them. Help them when possible to participate and explore things at their own pace.

• Be as honest as possible about what you say to intuitively gifted children. They will sense your honesty and will respond readily and sincerely without judgment. They do not have to know every emotional problem or nuance in your life; simply express yourself as clearly as possible to them. If you are confused or unclear about your feelings on a matter that involves them, they may misinterpret your confusion unless you express it to them. Do not be afraid to be your incomplete, imperfect self. They will love you for it.

• Do not encourage intuitively gifted children to be or act like adults. With insights and feelings often more mature than those of many of their peers, they will generally gravitate toward people physically older. Their pronounced sensitivities, intelligence, and emotional depths are a refreshing comfort to adults, who may unknowingly treat them as close friends or confidants. They are still physically children and may become overburdened by issues and responsibilities they cannot handle emotionally. They need to be appreciated for their gifts but be active and take part in the same activities as any other children.

• Be creative in devising new and challenging ways to teach and communicate ideas and knowledge and intellectually stimulate intuitively gifted children. Using your own gut reactions and intuitive and creative abilities, explore ways to encourage and educate them. They will participate eagerly and appreciate your efforts.

• If children are continually hyperactive for no known psychological or physiological reason, make special efforts to find creative outlets and activities that interest them. Encourage physical activity within their day so that they can release tension in ways that suit their needs. Extend playtime a few extra minutes before study. Incorporate other interests or talents of theirs when difficult lessons are planned.

• If intuitively gifted children have a hard time retaining information, look for creative ways they can use their innate talents to acquire more meaningful study habits. Discuss the total idea or concept of a lesson, story, or project. Suggest visual cues that may help them recall important information. Let them participate with you in the process so they can feel a sense of achievement and satisfaction.

• If intuitively gifted children are exceptionally withdrawn, find creative activities that encourage them to use their empathic sensitivity. Find ways of including them in decision making and explore their view of things without force or success/failure incentive.

• If children have trouble concentrating, feel too pressured to maintain focus, or are emotionally or physically overwhelmed by everything around them, create a relaxing atmosphere where they can move around. Help them practice Releasing Tension or Relaxation so they can call upon these techniques at will, to help them find their own ways to regain focus.

Every family, town, nation, or world is as productive and good as its people. Throughout world history there have always been special people who have listened to their dreams, believed their inner feelings, followed their intuitive responses, and helped and inspired humanity to widen its conventional wisdom. Those individuals came from many backgrounds. They brought new ideas and methods to progressively change our lives. They found cures for diseases and introduced technology and new ways of expression. They believed in more than what was physically known or seen or heard. Trusting their own intuition and believing in their inspired insights, they encouraged others to be daring and visualize new horizons.

Taking an active and creative approach to problems that intuitively gifted children experience can open a broader view for them about their world and their own potential. Helping intuitively gifted children to find their way in a technological, intellectually oriented society may one day give back to that society a great invention, idea, or individual to benefit the human family. With simple loving and understanding anyone can help nurture the sensitively brilliant talents of intuitively gifted children.

"Julie painted this picture. Do you believe it? Look at the incredible detail. I don't know where she gets it from. My husband and I can't even draw a straight line!"

"He runs, he plays basketball, AND he can sing? Where did you get this child?"

"Robby wrote this incredible story for school. Even the teacher said she was amazed. He hardly even talks in class."

All children bring the creativity of their souls to a physical learning place. Creativity is a part of their natural way of being. Little children often sing to themselves, perform a dance, act out a character of their own invention spontaneously, with or without an appreciative audience. Creativity is a fundamental way in which they learn about things long before they learn logic and social training.

Many children who are highly creative are also highly intuitive. They develop their talents at very early ages. Such children communicate freely with their muses, see pictures and designs where others do not, have an innate sense of musical timing and phrasing, write with wisdom that defies their age.

All too often the intuitive abilities they use in the creative process are rejected rather than nurtured and only their finished products are tangibly rewarded. The unspoken message is that inspiration is not valuable. Creativity is not valid without extraordinary tangible results. An end product is the only important result. There is no conscious effort or interest in the way in which a child paints a picture, sings a song, finds inspiration, or brings out the best in people. Not acknowledging children's intuitive talents as a part of their creative process often impedes their growth as artistic children. They learn proven remedial techniques rather than explore their own innovations; they follow limited suggestion rather than expanding their boundaries. Their "intangible" insights and urges become repressed and structured, inhibiting children's spontaneous creativity, leaving them feeling unhappy, temperamental, and frustrated. Without a foundation based on what they intrinsically know, they become hesitant and less likely to try new experiences.

Highly empathetic and sensitive, they may be told by teachers or parents their way of creating or what they create doesn't make sense, is silly or stupid, or should follow set views or techniques. They may not be emotionally secure enough to reject what others say and plunge ahead with their own vision. They may withdraw, lose confidence, become disillusioned about the talents that were once so exciting to them.

It is common for people to think of exceptionally creative children as those who are talented in the arts. Creativity in children manifests in other ways as well, but those ways are often disregarded. It is not uncommon for intuitively talented children to solve emotional or physical problems in innovative ways. They may conceptually know how to build or reorder mechanical gadgets, be good with their hands, and invent uncanny objects. They may improvise computer games, be exceptional debaters or communicators, or innovative thinkers. They may naturally excel at theoretical math or physics, or political strategy. They may be able to organize a game, an event, a family outing with efficiency and caring for all concerned. They may give sound advice and know innately how to care for others, shouldering life burdens adults are not handling. Children's creativity may be quite exceptional in everyday living experiences.

Children are born with their invisible talents. Adults' main focus should be to give them the support and freedom to explore those talents. Whether they are searching for ways to solve problems, come to conclusions, explore their environment, interact socially, or discover their voice, art, or language, they need to travel their own path. If they show an inclination toward drawing and sculpting, show them how to find meaning in the process. They will innately be far more intrigued by the methodology than by what they physically produce. They bring this potential to all their experiences. If they are socially creative, with encouragement they can use similar talents in studying math and science. Tapping into their visual talents can help them learn their more difficult subjects. Incorporating their intellectual creative abilities may enable them to understand their deep feelings and emotions. Their athletic drive and focus techniques may be used in other areas as well.

Creative children are usually precocious readers, writers, artists, musicians, mathematicians, scientists, and counselors who might have trouble with those same skills once they enter school. In a structured classroom setting, their natural process may be overlooked, forsaken to conform to regimented learning, or stifled due to emphasis on a top grade or performance. They may lack support at home for nurturing their talents and the space or time to explore these talents in their own way.

The connection between children's intuitive and creative talents may go unnoticed, limiting their view of themselves, their talents, and the multidimensional world around them. Children who are intuitively gifted as well as highly creative may:

• Be very aware of and intrigued by physical experiences. They readily explore new and unusual physical experiences and show strong desire and curiosity to interact with their environment.

• Openly experience the intangible world inside themselves without feeling self-conscious or losing their sense of physical reality. They will feel as much at home with their visualizations and conceptual reasoning as they do with any physical discovery or interaction.

• Exhibit a greater than usual depth of perception and feeling of beauty, love, harmony, and understanding. They will feel comfortable with universal feelings that live on a deep level inside us.

• Think for themselves without losing their capacity to empathize with the people around them. They will feel free to invent and investigate without cutting themselves off socially.

• Communicate freely both verbally and telepathically. They will feel equally attuned to both physical and nonphysical means of exchange.

In societies that value technological advancement to achieve material gains, creative children can often feel misplaced. If their creative insights and talents do not correspond to modern rational thought, they feel left out. Ironically, they are seen as dreamers and yet may be the visionaries who create the next technological innovations. They may be the underachievers, unable to perform simple rote exercises, but test beyond the norm on conceptual achievement exams. They may be intellectually advanced but compromise their innovative thinking for the goal of winning or getting ahead of others. They need to be reminded of their balance in this physical world. Their visions are worthy. Their dreams can be applied to physical goals. Exceptional creative intuitive children are living reminders that for every innovation in our world there were inventors, designers, creators who used their uncanny gifts to show society anything is possible.

Prodigies

Wolfgang Amadeus Mozart composed minuets before the age of four.

Fréderíc Chopin gave concerts at age nine.

Albrecht Dürer created his famous self-portrait at age thirteen.

The Brontë sisters, Charlotte, Emily, and Anne, wrote novels as children.

Blaise Pascal formulated his own geometry as a young boy when he was deprived of books on mathematics.

Prodigies are viewed by Western society as gifts, freaks of nature, or both. In early times they were touted from village to village, invited to kingly courts to show their uncanny talents. Today they are invited to appear on talk shows, written about in exploitative magazines, and tested by scientists.

It is believed that the incredible talents of most prodigies are fully developed before the age of four. Prodigious children come into this world at birth readily able to use highly developed skills and exhibit them in full abundance. One theory is that these highly developed talents, whether artistic or intellectual, are carryovers from past lives.

Such precocious and highly intuitive children enter a physical world of many contradictions. They are often made to focus solely on their extraordinary talents and not allowed to learn like other young children. They are recognized and rewarded for only one exceptional part of themselves, at the cost of the development of the other aspects of themselves. In the 1800s prodigies were even paraded across the United States like sideshow freaks. Still not allowed to fall short of society's expectations, today these children continually work hard to prove themselves. Often deprived of regular daily social contact with other children, they are surrounded by adult expectations. Filled with loving wisdom and emotionally sensitive beyond their physical age, too often they become prisoners of a singular well-developed talent. They often feel guilty for having talents that would take others years of training to acquire. They feel inadequate to deal directly with mundane parts of their personal lives.

Mozart, a brilliant composer at an early age, is said to have suffered a lifetime of difficulty reconciling a superbly mature talent with emotional immaturity. Most prodigies suffer similar problems. Held aloft in an adult world that applauds their awe-inspiring talents, they are still young children emotionally and psychologically. Even with uncanny intuition, they lack the tangible knowledge and emotional development to understand their physical lives and daily interactions. Prodigious children may be able to create fine works of art but may not know how to deal with social behavior. They may find it difficult to verbalize their deep feelings without shared communication. They may develop psychological defenses to protect their sensitivities in other areas of their lives. They may, in fact, see themselves only in terms of their extraordinary talent and may use it to gain love, approval, affection, and trust.

Regardless of the particular area of brilliance, children with advanced talents share similar intuitive characteristics. Such children are:

- Extremely sensitive
- Self-defined at an early age
- Advanced in their talents and thinking processes
- Mature in their knowledge but emotionally confused
- Imaginative and quick to understand things
- Filled with curiosity, especially about their field
- Precocious in speech and vocabulary

In order to develop fully, prodigious children, like all other children, need intimate contact with peers, reinforcement, discipline, and encouragement. They need acceptance of their special talents but also freedom to fail and prosper without recrimination. A compassionate caring environment enables them to further use and develop their special talents so they can indeed feel balanced and loved as they share their special gifts with society.

Physically, Mentally, and Emotionally Challenged Children

When Brian, age seven, was dying of a brain tumor he greeted his doctor one day by announcing that he had not eaten his dinner dessert. Perplexed, the doctor asked why. Brian smiled and told the doctor he was waiting for the surprise cookie the doctor had saved in his office for him.

Blind since birth, Debby, age three, always knew when her father was about to arrive home from work. Being a truck driver, he had no set schedule. But regardless of the time or day, she was always at the front door to greet him when he came home.

Amy speaks in sign. One night she dreamed about her brother, James, who died in a car accident before she was born. In that dream James and Amy spoke easily together as if they had been talking for many years.

In certain cultures children born with physical differences and limitations are looked upon as special due to their reliance on divine powers early in life. In Samoa, hunchbacks were thought to be gifted with spiritual powers. In Melanesia, children born with extra fingers or toes were thought to possess great magical talent. Blind people have often been treated as visionaries who owe their illuminating wisdom to their "unseen" connections. In some African tribes, physically challenged children are respected and taught in the ways of the shaman.

Physical limitations do not diminish or limit children's intuitive abilities. Children physically challenged since birth suffer no impairment of their sixth sense. Such thinking is reinforced by early parapsychological tests, done in the 1930s, involving intuitive abilities in blind children. Tests for Telepathy done with blind and sighted children have shown results that vary according to the particular child rather than the limits of his eyesight. In addition, children who have been blind since birth have scored as high or higher in intuitive testing than children who were once sighted or have always had physical sight.

Physically challenged children may be even more attuned to the use of their intuition to help themselves interact in life. Children unable to rely on motor functions or sight, hearing, speech, or other physical senses may naturally rely more on Telepathy, Clairvoyance, or intuitive reading for insight, knowledge, and daily communication.

Blind children will acutely develop their sense of smell and touch and hearing but will also rely on their Clairvoyance and Mediumship. Their vision of situations and their intuition about people will be as finely tuned as their hearing. These special intuitive abilities help to provide direction and protection. Without physical vision to guide their decisions, they learn to depend on their gut reactions. They may sense the moods of people before approaching them. They may envision their environment along with using their physical senses.

Deaf children respond more quickly and effectively because they are highly sensitive to motion and action. They are able to read people beyond their physical expressions and often intuit what a person has to say before the person actually speaks. As they read lips or body language deaf children also sense the unspoken feelings that voices betray. They often sense people or danger approaching, and they intuit the moods of others. They use their sixth sense to listen deeply to what a person has to say beyond words. It has been speculated that telepathic communication, if able to be physically demonstrated, would be similar to the sign language of deaf people.

Children confined to wheelchairs or beds or who endure terminal illnesses are also highly sensitive to their environment. They read the moods of people without moving or speaking. It is often the dying child who senses and calms the fears of people around him with the wisdom and compassion of his soul. His strong empathetic nature allows others to share this deeper loving and intuitive level of understanding with him.

Physically challenged children unable to respond to situations physically learn to trust and rely on their gut responses. They intuitively sense the fears and other inner feelings of people who teach and help them. They can read the sincerity in people and respond emotionally. They often rely on their intuitive abilities to communicate with family members and health care professionals whose physical assistance they need. If unable to speak verbally, they revert to communicating telepathically to express themselves. Young siblings often intercede and translate when adults do not understand a physically challenged child. Physically challenged children rely on their sixth sense to figure out ways to perform daily tasks. Even when they are unable to experience their environment outside their home or hospital or nursing center physically, their clairvoyant visions and dreams enable them to revisit places they have been or experience new places and situations. Although unable to respond physically to the immediate feelings or actions of others, they may still intuitively know and experience those feelings on deep levels within themselves. Studies recently done on people in comas have found that although they cannot respond visibly they do respond intuitively to voice, touch, and others' presence.

Physically challenged children face more bodily impediments, emotional frustration, and social ostracism than other children in a physically active world. Their intuitive abilities help them not only to achieve their potential but to gain self-esteem despite their limitation. Finding intuitive ways to explore and use their innate abilities enables them to do more and develop other levels of themselves, gain self-respect, appreciate their own beauty, and be more excited about themselves and their world. Integrating the use of both their intuitive talents and their physical talents allows physically challenged children to feel less dependent and more capable of handling themselves without inhibition.

Since Joe was an infant, his father had physically abused him. When he was two, his parents separated. Joe knows when his father, a freelance journalist, is about to visit, regardless of the time of day. Hours before his father's unexpected arrival Joe clings to his mother. If he is sleeping, he will awaken before his father drives up the street and opens the front door.

Janice, away at school, began having nightmares and crying spells about her parents' separation two years before her mother found out her father was having an extramarital affair.

Pablo knew the answers to two complicated math problems on a surprise test even though he was failing math. When asked, he could not explain how he arrived at the answers.

*Eddie is mentally challenged. He cannot feed himself eas-
ily and forgets how to do a simple task even if he has just performed it. Yet he almost always knows what his mother is
thinking at the same time she is thinking it and when the
school bus is going to be late.*

In medieval Europe, emotionally and mentally challenged
children were thought to be wicked. They were considered sor-
cerers possessing supernatural secrets and talents. Today these
children are often poor students, socially rejected by their peers,
and thought to be less capable than other children their age.

Children with organic mental dysfunction from birth or as
the result of an accident often rely, like infants, on sensing people and using telepathic communication to convey their needs
and desires. The more "childlike" severely mentally challenged
children appear, the more they tend to rely on their innate intuitive capabilities. They sense peoples' moods and insecurities
without thinking. Their unconditional loving and strong sense
of spiritual connection enable them to open themselves emotionally to others. Their innate curiosity about the world allows
them spontaneously to achieve insight and knowledge in their
explorations. With limited speech and mental intelligence, such
children can still convey their needs, hopes, or frustrations non-
verbally. They often react intensely to the thoughts or feelings of
others, sense danger, and can tell right from wrong in foreign situations on a primary intuitive level. They also, like infants, can
acutely sense the energy in a room and the deeper loving of people when many adults do not.

These children with limited mental and verbal skills, although possibly more refined in their intuitive sensibilities, find
themselves isolated and rejected by society. Put in special programs at schools focused solely on intellectual learning, they are
segregated from other children at playtime. They cannot compete

in classroom situations and often have a hard time with methods and tools that do not incorporate all of their abilities. All too often, mentally challenged children begin to doubt their initial gut reactions and seek approval and acknowledgment from others whom they see as mentally powerful. They seek support and explanation from people who ignore intuitive avenues of expression and reward only intellectual methods of relating to the world. In such an environment mentally challenged children have no peers, no support, and little potential.

Although there are vast differences in mental development between severely mentally challenged children and others, it is interesting that telepathic tests done with both groups have shown similar results. Scores were equal in many instances. Confused and frustrated by their lack of verbal skills and mental acuity, these children are taught to focus away from their natural telepathic, mediumistic, and clairvoyant talents that aid them in learning and communication. Long neglected for what they cannot be, mentally challenged children can be regarded and admired for the attributes and talents they do have. Encouraging them to use their intuitive talents can build self-esteem, help them discover new ways of learning, and aid in communication. Many of these children are capable of surpassing the limited expectations put upon them.

Contrary to popular belief, intellectually gifted children often have similar problems. Much admired in Western society for their mental brilliance, they may also suffer rejection, ostracism, and emotional neglect. Trained at an early age to focus on rational thought and mental potential, they quickly reject their innate talents and overcompensate by relying solely on their intelligence. Depending on their brain and dismissive of gut reactions, they begin to find it difficult to make incidental decisions without thinking. They become less psychologically and emotionally developed. Struggling for intellectual brilliance, they often block the deeper intuitive impressions that surface without rational thought. They suffer socially for this imbalance, unable to sense things other children understand, less able to share themselves emotionally without mental justification, unable to experience the wonder of living without mental explanation. Children who have developed their intellect may be rewarded in class for being able to solve the most complicated mathematical equation or write the most detailed history report but may be unable to relate to others or use their common sense in everyday situations. Encouraged to recognize their intellect but allowed to value their innate ability to sense and read people, explore dreams, and communicate without thinking, they will be able to enhance their mental learning and lead a more integrated life outside the classroom.

Emotionally challenged children with no tested organic dysfunction create their own set of problems. Often reactive to others, they feel things so deeply they cannot express them. Emotionally out of balance, they have a hard time coping with the problems of others and the world around them. They may be highly intelligent but so disruptive, distracted, or distraught they are put in learning disabled classes. They may not be able to complete their homework, are often withdrawn and inactive, or act out in class. Overwhelmed by their emotions, they may be too inhibited or confused to explore any of their other gifts.

Highly intuitively sensitive or mediumistic children have emotional difficulty responding clearly to their immediate environment and social situations. They struggle to separate themselves from the feelings of others and their own inner desires. They can become abusive, resentful, angry, scared, fearful, anxious, or depressed. Outwardly they may appear similar in actions to children with physiological or biochemical problems, but inwardly they are very different. With no medical history of emotional imbalance their moods and emotions may change quickly for any number of reasons.

Renée was three years old. Often agitated, she seemed to have a lot of difficulty socializing with other children. Her mother took her to a psychologist for evaluation. Medical tests showed she had no medical or physiological disorder. The psychologist worked with her about the obvious cause for her emotional discomfort: the divorce of her parents. Some days she seemed fine. Others she became enraged. The mental deductions were obvious. Her outer world had shifted and she was having a tough time readjusting to the changing family environment around her. Then one day, in the psychologist's office, something very different happened.

At the beginning of her session Renée was unduly hostile and belligerent. She did not want to participate in any discussion or activity. She was adamant about not cooperating, yelling at anyone who approached. Her mother could not pinpoint any incident that day that might have sparked such behavior.

At the end of the rather frustrating session a stranger, a person using an adjoining office, entered the room. Renée was hostile and angry toward her as well. In an offhanded gesture, the woman invited Renée to see her office, knowing the mother needed to speak with the psychologist. Without hesitation, and in a way that was completely out of character, Renée walked casually through the doorway into the other office. As soon as she entered the room her behavior changed. Without any discussion she became pleasant, comfortable, and happy, freely examining everything in the office without fear or hostility. When her mother stepped into the office, Renée hesitated, then announced she did not want to leave. She told the person, "I like your home."

> *Trying to make sense of the vast difference in the child's behavior, the psychologist later realized that the patient who had been in his office previous to Renée had been very emotional, irate over a business deal gone sour. Renée had entered the room after his session and had immediately begun to act out in an uncontrollable manner.*

Was Renée a little girl filled with her own pent-up emotions? Had she intuitively responded to the energy in the room? Or had her intuitive reaction simply added to her own emotional situation? When Renée was removed from that physical environment, her emotional state stabilized.

Such intuitively sensitive children often spontaneously respond in extremes. They are often categorized as underachievers or troubled children and made to feel unworthy: they are punished, embarrassed, ridiculed, or ostracized for behavior they cannot control. Extraordinarily intuitively sensitive children, placed in a classroom filled with the energies and emotions of other children, will respond: they may be unable to sit still for long periods of time; they may become inordinately shy and withdrawn; they may keep losing focus on their lessons or become distracted when being given direction; they may be moody or emotional. Such children are often described as good kids who keep having problems. They react without malice or forethought. These emotionally intuitive children who are disruptive in behavior to themselves and others are invariably put in the same category as children who do have severe emotional problems or psychological disabilities, and are treated as such.

Incredibly empathic by nature, many emotionally intuitive children unconsciously sense and react to underlying feelings in family members. They can sense a parent or sibling's inner needs or desires but remain incapable of helping. They will know when someone doesn't believe in them or is afraid of dealing with them. This causes these children to feel resentful, like failures, and disappointed in themselves. They may respond to the rejection of classmates but be too sensitive to verbalize their emotions. Since the children do not understand the reasons for their extreme feelings or how to work through them, the feelings accumulate, causing them to become even more emotionally hyperreactive. During family crisis situations—when contentious parents get divorced, a father or mother is drinking or taking drugs, a family member dies or is sick, or there is physical or emotional abuse in the family between parents—such children respond deeply and often more openly than others. They not only feel their natural emotional reactions and responses but also intuitively sense the responses of everyone else involved.

Afraid to voice their odd perceptions to adults who may already be agitated, confused, or insecure, empathically intuitive children learn at an early age to distrust and ignore their initial impressions. When these emotions have no release and become pent up they provoke fear and guilt. Such emotionally challenged children often try to regain their natural balance of energy by withdrawing from situations and keeping their feelings to themselves. They may seek reinforcement through people who are not part of the emotional situation. They may strive to become overachievers, hoping to please adults and compensate for their feelings of inadequacy. They may become manipulative in order to gain power and avoid their fears.

Intuitively sensitive children know when they are told the truth no matter how bad it may be. Like all children they learn to adjust and deal with physical situations. What they do not know how to do is accept the confused emotions, actions, or thinking of people they love. Uncertain behavior fuels their own uncertain emotional reactions to unfamiliar situations. Without understanding of their intuitive responses, they become confused and distrustful of their own feelings. They may act out against those who create this disturbance or become scapegoats for emotionally stressful family situations. They may stop communicating altogether, trusting no one—including themselves.

Adults who trust their own gut responses to people and situations can help sensitive children begin to understand their emotional boundaries with people. Intuitively knowing them and communicating your feelings clearly without forcing children to become emotionally responsible adults goes a long way toward relieving some of their emotional load. Honest communication will help them sort through their own feelings and yours. Sense their moods before you decide to talk with them. Trust your responses to know when they are emotionally available for discussion. Even if they do not respond strongly to your words, do not think they did not hear you. Keenly listening on an intuitive level, they may be overwhelmed by emotions at that moment. They will respond at a later time, demonstrating through their behavior that they understood every word you said.

The incorporation of visual communication through drawings or telling stories can help small children too overwhelmed with emotions to explain what they are feeling. Simple emotional impressions can be a starting point to help children describe feelings without fear. Rather than sitting down specifically to talk in a confronting manner, speak when you are both relaxed and able to relate fears, anger, hopes, and feelings without judgment. Allow children who are upset to release emotions they may not be able to verbalize by crying or running or simply being with you.

The most important thing emotionally intuitive children need is trust. No matter how tense, overwhelmed, or upset they become, if they sense a giving heart, an open mind, a kind touch, they will be willing to share their inner feelings. An open heart is more important to them than all the rationalizations in the world for their behavior. Honest feelings will enable them to find balance in their immediate environment to help them sort out their confusions. Without fear or recrimination children so richly sensitive can use their intuitive abilities to open healing doors to feelings and places inside them that have been protectively closed but never truly locked.

There are no easy solutions to any of these problems. All children are a mix of their intuitive, mental, and emotional components. Keep things simple. Children respond to things on a basic level. Psychological counseling and physical as well as emotional support can help. Learning to understand and trust their own intuitive perceptions lets them validate themselves and begin to trust what they know and feel without regret, recrimination, or misunderstanding.

Whether children are emotionally challenged, intellectually gifted, or mentally or physically challenged, they can use their intuitive talents to help rather than hinder them in overcoming social, mental, or emotional obstacles to better connect with the human family.

Common Questions and Answers

Are all children intuitively gifted?

All children have intuitive abilities, but not all children are intuitively gifted. As with any other talent, the degree of intuitive talent depends on individual potential, desire for development, and practice. All children with abundant intuitive talents should be allowed the opportunity to explore and develop them at their own rate.

How can intuitively gifted children use their unique intuitive talents in the physical world?

By being open to their talents, they will begin to find ways in which those talents can be beneficial to them and those around them in their daily life. Their sensitivity and empathy will help them to understand their environment and connect with the feelings of other people. Their sensing and intuitive reading ability will help them to choose people and opportunities that can be beneficial and conducive to their learning and sharing. Their creativity will lead them toward innovation and progress and stimulate others. Their dreams and visualizations will give insight toward problem solving and creative thinking. Their sense of universal spiritual connections will enable them to feel and share with others on deeper, meaningful levels beyond physical boundaries.

Are most intuitively gifted children being placed in learning disabled programs? Are all children in learning disabled programs intuitively gifted?

As diverse as children are, so are their problems. Many children in learning disabled programs have problems that are more physically or emotionally linked than intuitively related. Some children have both physical learning problems and intuitive-related problems. There are others, however, whose intuitive-associated problems are mistakenly attributed to other causes. And then there are many intuitively gifted children, although not in special classes, who may be underachievers or overachievers who suffer psychologically or emotionally because of their special talents. Such classifications are not easily made. Rather than place all children who have difficulty learning in learning disabled programs, it might be beneficial to include alternatives to mainstream classes, such as practicing exercises that address the specific needs and problems of intuitively gifted children.

Where do prodigies get their abundance of talent at such an early age?

Prodigies bring their highly developed creative abilities with them into this life as a part of their soul or nonphysical self. Such special and well-developed talents are often thought to have progressed to a mature level during past lives. Talents such as these are not accidental, and children who possess them need to cultivate their talents and address the ways in which related problems can be alleviated.

What can you do for children who show no interest in creative activities?

Creativity does not necessarily apply solely to the arts—writing, acting, singing, dancing, and painting. Children can be creatively talented in many other ways. They may be creative in their thinking, in arranging their room, in mechanical ways, in dealing with people, or in social interactions. Creativity in children needs to be reinforced and nurtured so that they can feel good about their natural gifts without fear of judgment or rejection. Children may become reticent, reluctant to experience or develop their creative abilities, if they are segregated or forced into an exclusive area. Be willing to acknowledge the many ways to express creativity.

Are emotionally challenged children always intuitively gifted?

Not all children who have emotional problems are intuitively gifted. Those children who are intuitively gifted and suffer from emotional problems tend to be more highly reactive, withdrawn, or sensitive to external stimulation than most children.

Do physically challenged children have a more highly developed sixth sense than other children?

Physically challenged children tend to practice and use their nonphysical talents more than other children. There are children who are not physically challenged who also use and practice their natural intuitive abilities. All children, regardless of physical limitation, have their own intuitive talents at their disposal to develop, enjoy, and use to make their lives fuller.

Should emotionally unstable children be taken to therapists or health care professionals, or to intuitive spiritual counselors?

It is important to remember that all children have different problems and to consider all options and possibilities when seeking care and help. Before consulting a spiritual counselor, however, it is a good idea to see a medical doctor or psychologist to eliminate other physical and psychological causes. Consulting a trained therapist or health care professional need not rule out the help of a professional intuitive or spiritual counselor. Each, in fact, may complement the other, just as the body complements the soul. One may be able to give insight and help the physical body, the other able to give insight and affect the soul. When exploring treatment for a child, consideration should be given to all levels so that the child can achieve a healthy and continuing balance.

6

Into the Twenty-first Century

Guns and Roses

Children in the modern world are besieged. They worry about a deteriorating environment. They live within shrinking families or with single parents or stepparents or in foster homes. They surf the Internet, interact through video games, eat junk food, and fear for their physical safety in school. More children than ever before are placed in learning disabled classes, are physically abused, seen by psychotherapists or psychiatrists, given prescription drugs. What will the future offer them? How will they manage to cope?

A group of intuitively talented middle-class teenagers recently got together to talk about their fears and hopes. Most but not all of these children were from single-parent or stepparent homes. They spoke openly about intuitively knowing their parents' personal problems and even their parents' worries about them. They felt their parents needed to work on their problems, couldn't communicate with them, and didn't try. They were upset that their parents "worked too much" and "didn't seem happy or together" in their lives. They talked about how they could read their teachers at school and know when they could slack off on schoolwork and when they had to pay attention in class. They knew when adults and friends were in bad moods and how far to push them emotionally.

After talking about personal issues they started talking about what was happening in America, of children killing other children in our schools:

> *"I think kids kill other kids because they feel so isolated and unhappy."*
> *"Kids can be really mean."*
> *"They don't feel like they belong."*
> *"Yeah. Kids can be so mean to each other."*
> *"It's hard to fit in."*
> *"Kids think they know a lot more but they're still kids."*
> *"They've got all this anger."*
> *"Yeah. But who would want to kill anybody?"*
> *"Especially people you know."*
> *"I don't know. They just feel left out, I guess."*
> *"They probably have a lot of rage inside them. About their lives in general."*
> *"Kids get into groups and they don't care about anyone else. Then it's too late."*
> *"I know some kids who could probably do that."*
> *"I don't."*
> *"Kids are messed up. So many kids are messed up."*
> *"Their parents should talk to them more."*
> *"Yeah, they should spend some time with them. Get involved with their lives."*
> *"But not too much!"*

"It's hard to solve something like that with just one answer. In an instant."

"It's a bigger problem."

"I think kids don't trust themselves enough. What they're feeling.

"They should trust their intuition. Like listen to themselves more."

"They'd know how to get out of bad situations."

"They'd know what to trust."

"Yeah, if they listened to their psychic intuition they'd understand more."

"They wouldn't kill other kids. That's for sure."

"They couldn't. Even if they were angry enough."

"Even if they thought about it."

"Yeah. They couldn't be violent and hurt anyone."

"Or themselves. They wouldn't cut themselves."

"If kids listened to their psychic feelings they could read the other people."

"They'd know what the other person was feeling at that exact moment."

"They'd feel their fear and they couldn't do it."

"They'd feel the other person was just as messed up as them."

"Yeah. It's like if you feel what another person is feeling at the same time you feel bad for them or sad or something."

"They'd feel the other kid's pain and not just their own."

"You can't kill someone you feel."

"I don't know. They wouldn't live happily ever after but they wouldn't kill each other."

Today's societies can clone baby sheep, create infants in test tubes, and save the arms and legs and hearts of children using medical technology, but they do not understand the children themselves. Times are different. Children are different in their attitudes and problems. The modern world that has made immense technological and psychological advances has yet to come to terms with the spiritual potential of its young. A world in which we are all interconnected by digital wires and codes has yet to come to grips with the innate invisible codes of its children. Children are bombarded with decisions, goals, rewards, problems, and stimuli that force them to be more than children in a world that does little to reinforce or sustain their natural inner balance. Educators and parents who are trained to deny their own intuitive talents—but who use them unwittingly nonetheless—ignore the need to explore the many possibilities of such talents in children. As a result, everyone suffers. Solutions for enabling children to achieve their total potential become limited. Allowing children to acknowledge and appreciate their inner wealth may not solve all of the world's problems they face but it will help equip them to find creative solutions they may not otherwise have known to be possible.

Intuitively gifted children come in all nationalities, shapes, and sizes. They look no different from other children. They have the same dreams and hopes and aspirations. Teaching them to believe there are only physical explanations in life limits not only their self-development but the development of the societies in which they live. It has been said that children hold the voices of the future, but who is listening?

During World War II many European children—in air raid shelters or in their own homes—anticipated bombings and voiced their fears before the bombs fell. Their intuitive insights and warnings were disregarded. In fact, the children were seen and treated as hysterical, unruly, and bad for the morale of the others around them. At the time, little was said about these incidents. It was not until years later that people began to validate and connect the "interesting coincidences" of the children's intuitive feelings and the explosions that soon followed.

Western children may live in a very rationally focused world but their childhood holidays and customs still allow for the supernatural, albeit with a modern commercial twist. Halloween, or Saimhain, a time for communing with the spirit world, is widely celebrated; children dress like ghosts, goblins, witches, and other supernatural beings, visit haunted houses, listen to ghost stories. Santa Claus, a mythical friend, and his reindeer watch over boys and girls all year to see if they have been good and deliver presents on Christmas Eve while they are sleeping. The Easter bunny hides colored eggs in the spring and brings candy and treats. A mystical spirit called the Tooth Fairy visits young children's bedrooms at night to give them secret comfort over the loss of first teeth by leaving a surprise gift under their pillows. In all cultures and throughout history children celebrate the supernatural in positive ways.

The portrayal of children with a sixth sense in movies, television, books, and magazines is at odds with nature and society. Little boys see dead people and suffer for it. Girls start fires. Boys destroy other children and scare adults with their uncanny abilities. Children worship at unholy sites, communicate with otherworldly creatures, and change in appearance to become wicked little demons or witches.

Most children with exceptional intuitive talents have no desire to become witches or demons or even professional seers or psychics. Staying in touch with these deeply ingrained talents can help such a child grow up to be an intuitive doctor or sensitive teacher, a caring mother or father, a gardener with an incredible green thumb. Perhaps there should be public forums where families and children can openly discuss their intuitive talents and explore their problems.

Although governments have acknowledged the existence of psychic abilities, their programs to examine these talents have been targeted for use in military and security matters. The Soviets also studied the use of Kirlian photography (a process in which a high-frequency electric field is applied to an object so that the object's characteristic pattern of luminescence—its aura—can be captured on film) in training Olympic athletes; the images were used to pinpoint muscle groups that needed more conditioning. Parapsychologists and scientists sporadically study psychic talents in children but their tests are primitive and have no way to truly quantify the results. Batteries of tests given to children in scientific labs focus on only two of the eight types of intuitive abilities children possess: Telepathy and Clairvoyance; children who are extremely talented in other types of psychic abilities have their talents ignored. The repetitive tests drastically limit the results for highly intuitive children, who are unusually creative, conceptual rather than rote, and spontaneous. These children, placed in austere settings, soon become bored, tired, or mentally blocked, and this stops the natural flow of their intuitive impressions. Conducting tests in comfortable and relaxed environments will help release the full potential of children's talents.

Another problem with current tests is the artificial separation of talents. Intuitively gifted children do not understand the boundaries of each individual gift because they use all their skills fluidly, not separating one from another. So to test these children for an isolated talent in a sterile laboratory would be like testing dancers for only one dance movement, athletes for only one phase of their run, singers for one note, mathematicians for one mathematical operation. Highly talented, sensitive children feel inhibited by the great expectations they sense from scientists. Empathetic and wishing to please, they lose the natural and relaxed focus that allows their intuitive abilities to flow.

The Next One Thousand Years

We are a global community that surpasses the Internet.
We are a universal community connected by our souls.

What will the world look like one thousand years from now? Perhaps we will live on the moon or in other galaxies. Life expectancy may rise to over two hundred years. Cars may really fly. Food may become nutritious pellets and houses may be virtual shelters to be taken wherever we go. Disease may be nonexistent and new forms of energy may fuel the world. The future world may be so different from what we physically know that we can only dream of the possibilities.

One thing above all others will remain constant—the coexistence of bodies and souls. Bodies will be born and die and souls will live on. Regardless of how physically advanced our global or intergalactic society may become, the sixth sense of children will not go away. Serving as living reminders, they show us that we are eternally and tangibly connected to something greater than our physical lives, far beyond our physical accomplishments. Every infant who enters every physical society and culture continues to spiritually enrich the quality of our lives. Infants are living echoes of our souls, the spiritual legacy in a world of stress and confusion that renews wonder, communion, love, harmony, and beauty. This indelible echo is heard and felt in the everyday laughter and loving hearts of children.

The presence of children in anyone's life requires amazing change, of getting used to schedules, caretaking, finances, long-term goals, and altered lifestyles. The daily emotional adjustments of rearing children transform us: we become more responsible, responsive, attentive, and kind. Invisible changes take place in us as well: intuition is heightened, telepathic communication is experienced, unconditional loving is practiced. Children help restore life to the ill, hope to the troubled, and youth to the elderly in their unspoken interactions with them.

Children serve as benign reminders to adults that they, too, have a wealth of intuitive talents. In the company of children adults are free to drop their defenses and regain their inner balance. Children help us return to the fundamental feelings of the soul. They unabashedly hold the magic antidote of spiritual loving when everything else fails. They crawl into our laps when we let no one approach us, sit beside us without explanation, take our hands to feel us, and enter our hearts to heal. They remind us that we can always be loved, that we are worth nurturing, and that we are capable of affection. The sweet gentle unconditional caring of children helps heal problems, physical distress, fear, and frustration. This gentle healing reaches beyond the impulses of the skin. It returns us to the core of our spiritual being.

Keeping the Intuitive Child Within Adults

"You know, I used to be psychic when I was little."

"I still remember my imaginary playmate's name. But I don't know how to talk to him anymore."

"I've always thought I lived in France in another time. I don't know why. As a kid I had dreams of living there even though I didn't even know where it was on a map."

"I don't like those butterflies I get in my stomach when something's about to go wrong."

"I just had a feeling about it. I can't explain it."

"All my friends come to me for advice. I don't know where it comes from but it's usually right."

"This stuff scares me. Especially when I'm right!"

You need not have, or live with, or be around children to be intuitive. All adults were intuitive as children. Many adults were intuitively gifted children. They still remember predicting events that came to pass; reading people accurately; giving what turned out to be the right advice; performing healings on pets; talking to spirits, deceased relatives, and imaginary playmates; and having dreams that came true. Every time adults retell stories about intuitive childhood experiences, a smile invariably appears on their faces. They become excited. Then the moment passes and they move on to become a seriously "responsible" adult again. They have learned their physical lessons well.

As the newest members of the human tribe, children enter this physical world spiritually attuned. They use their natural balance to function; to sense beauty, wisdom, loving; and to appreciate the deeper meanings of things. They rely on their intuition to help them explore the world in interesting ways.

As children continue to physically develop they become more attuned to their physical environment and routine. They wake and sleep according to imposed schedules. They eat at prescribed times. They focus on the demands and goals of those who have been physically focused before them. They rely on their mental thoughts. Children program their behavior to fit in and deal with the specifics of their everyday life. They conform their feelings to seek out social reinforcement. They have no time to think about what is happening. They focus on what they think they want or need. They have places to go to, deadlines to meet, and people who need them. They try to be responsible, to work hard, and ultimately to become successful adults and raise a family, own nice houses, drive expensive cars, and send their children to fine schools.

Yet at moments in their adult lives feelings arise that do not conform to what they have been taught. Experiences that are not "normal" do not go away. Sometimes they just predict something out of the blue and it happens. Often a vivid dream stirs them from sleep. It jolts them when they know what people are thinking and that someone might know them more deeply than they know themselves.

No matter how many years people live on this planet or how much they deny their inner talents, their intuitive abilities remain. The strongest psychological defenses cannot deny the strong bond between body and soul, a constant connection to all of life. This union is often felt as a simple moment of wonder, an instant of insight, an encounter with beauty. The feeling that arises in all adults is exactly the same as it was when they were children. This deeper communion is like a dream waiting to be recognized again. Touching upon and remembering this union can occur at any time in a person's day and life, whether he or she is three, twenty-three, or eighty-three. The potential for body-and-soul balance inside each adult is available, regardless of psychological defenses. These deeper inner feelings do not go away and only increase with awareness.

It is easy to return to that inner core without restricting your physical knowledge or maturity. Trust your Feeling Response in daily decisions and experiences. Pay attention to your dreams. Listen to insights that pop into your head without forethought or analysis. Try to read and sense the feelings of the people around you, including children and pets. Allow yourself to touch and be touched as you feel it. Allow thoughts to pass through your mind without judgment.

Becoming aware of intuition can be exciting and can open adults to new vistas and tap into natural and comfortable feelings. Rediscovering intuitive talents adds to your potential and development in life. Understand your mate, business partner, adversary, boss, potential lover a little better. Listen to impressions about goals and changes in work and life. Find meaning in moments that lead to new experiences. Intuition is not a magic pill but a natural return to self. Become a child in the best sense by appreciating the physical world of your body and all its richness and the world of the soul with its incredible wealth and depth.

Common Questions and Answers

What can schools and other public institutions do for intuitive children?

School is the place where children further develop their mental, emotional, creative, athletic, and social talents. It can also nurture intuitive talents to enhance the learning process, produce innovative programs, and instill a sense of pride in children about parts of themselves they naturally take for granted. When children are recognized for their many talents, including intuitive talents, they can then begin to explore and learn to integrate all parts of themselves to become more productive in their lives.

Should children be tested for intuitive abilities?

If tests are devised to enable science to understand intuitive abilities and aid children in the use of them, then such tests may benefit future generations. Children can provide suggestions and avenues of inquiry that may help scientists test their natural talents more effectively.

Can adults develop their sixth sense if they were not encouraged to do so during their childhoods?

Intuitive abilities can be developed at any time in people's lives. Unlike some physical talents, there is no prime time to develop intuitive talents. A willingness to be aware of such abilities and an openness to experiment and work toward attaining insights and impressions are all that is needed. Your intuitive abilities are already with you; with focus and freedom the perpetual development of them is yours.

Should intuitive abilities be addressed in public schools?

Intuitive abilities are used daily in public schools: the teacher who senses a child's problems when the child has been unable to verbalize them; the child who creates a picture or expresses himself in novel ways; the teacher or student who is reacting to the moods of others; the child who reaches out to another child to help and encourage his work without provocation. Acknowledging the unseen talents in children serves to make them visible working tools for better education and learning.

Who would best be able to teach children about their sixth sense? Parents? Teachers? Intuitives?

The title is not as important as the feelings. People who have children's best interests at heart and are open and loving and willing to learn about intuitive abilities will be good teachers. Some parents will relate to their children's intuitive abilities more easily than others because they acknowledge their own intuition. The same is true for teachers and for intuitives. People who are honest and willing to explore their own potential will be willing to help children explore theirs or to find those people trained in specific talents who can provide further help.

Why is there such a dramatic difference between the views of modern Western culture and those of primitive or past cultures regarding intuitive children?

The very physical and technological advances of modern Western society have emphasized tangible physical goals and rewards. All cultures rejoice in their young. However, primitive and past cultures have not lost a sense of the more spiritual focus of their ancestors or replaced it with physical advances. Western culture, although advanced in the comforts of physical life, needs to return to a balanced focus on both physical and nonphysical knowledge and being.

Children in
Their Own Voices

I don't know. My parents think I have problems. They think I'm weird. Strange. Whatever. They keep sending me to shrinks but they don't understand me. They think I'm crazy but I know I'm not. I see things sometimes. I know things that are true. I know when a teacher is lying to me. Then they get mad. I know that about my mom, too. When I tell her true things she gets really mad. I know what people are gonna say before they say it. I can see colors around my teachers. I know when some of my friends are unhappy. But I don't know what to do about it. It makes me upset.

My little brother is a pain but I know when my mom or dad is wrong about him. So I speak up for him and get in trouble. I like to paint but what I paint most people don't understand so I think I'm going to stop painting. Sometimes I don't feel like I'm from this world. I wish I had someone to talk to sometimes. It gets lonely.

—Christina, age 14

My sister Rachel died in a car accident three years ago. She visits me a lot in my dreams. First I thought I was just making it up. She tells me what it is like to be dead. She tells me she talks a lot to our family. She said she is with my grandparents and my Aunt Cathy who died of cancer. I tell my parents real direct stuff that she tells me that I never knew. It freaks them out so I don't tell them anymore. My friends would just laugh at me. But I know my sister is there.
—Danielle, age 13

Hi. I know stuff. Like last week I was goin' home and I knew somethin' was gonna come down in front of me. You could just feel it. You know what I mean? Sure enough one of my brother's friends got shot on the corner. Right there in front of me. More stuff came down. His posse was lookin' to settle the beef. I turned to Jason and told him they're gonna be lookin' for you. Get outta here. I just knew it was about him but I couldn't tell you why. Later I found out Jason had some old business with them. I know these things. Happens all the time. My street name is Majik.
—David, age 12

"A Special World"

I would like to live in a special world. It would be a world where people didn't hurt each other. Where flowers would grow and people would not kill animals. In this world everyone would be safe and have a home. People would help each other when they got sick just by touching them. Everyone would have a family and be able to have food to eat. We would learn to talk to our angels and they would help us with our homework. No one would be bad. If they were we would talk to them. And no one would ever die.

We would always know them and speak to them. Everyone would be happy and if they were sad we would help them.

My angel told me that I am special. And that I can make people feel better. Sometimes just like that I can touch somebody and they feel better. I did this with my little sister when she was sick. I do it with my mom and dad but they don't know it. They just feel better. When I was little I saw my grandma and my aunt in my dreams. They looked beautiful. They told me about the future. They told me what it's gonna be like. They said everybody will go places without cars. People won't need much food. And we will know what everyone is thinking. I would like to live in this world. In this world everyone is special. My grandmother told me that.

—Kerrie, age 6

One day I had a dream about my grandfather. I never knowed him but I saw a picture and I liked him a lot. I think he looks like me but everyone says he looks like my brother. Anyway in this dream my grandfather spoke to me. He said, "You are going to grow to be a fine man. You don't have to worry about nothing. You won't have cancer like I had." He smiled at me and I felt really good. Then I woke up. I couldn't go back to sleep because I was too excited and I guess a little scared. When I told my mother. It was her father. She looked at me as if I shot her or something. She said how did you know he died of cancer? Did I tell you? I said No. Did he die of cancer? Yes, she said, ten years before you were born. I said how was I supposed to know then? She wouldn't answer me. I think she was too upset.

—Felipe, age 11

I got angels. They come see me when nobody is around and they tickle me. I love them. Theyre real pretty. Some-

times I wish they would come to school with me but I only see them when Im real quiet. I hope they stay with me forever.

—LaToya, age 6

"*Fluffy My Cat*"

One day when Fluffy and I were sleeping we both dreamed that we could fly. We flew right out of the window and over the trees. It was so pretty. Fluffy wasn't scared because I was there. We didn't need wings or anything. We flew by the clouds and over to Jessica's house. Jessica was sleeping and she had on her yellow pajamas. Sometimes when I sleep over she wears them to bed. Fluffy didn't want to stay at Jessica's because she has a dog who isn't nice to cats. Then Fluffy and I flew to Grandma's. She never goes to sleep I guess because she was watching TV. It got boring so Fluffy and I went home and went to sleep.

—Nikki, age 8

My spiritual and psychic experiences began at a young age for me. One of the earliest examples of the deep spiritual side I have in me was connected with nature.

As a very young child, looking at a tree wasn't just thinking about climbing it or building a tree house. My mind would race back in time, looking inside of the tree. I could focus on its experiences, almost if feeling its past joys and pains. I would begin to have images of others that may have visited this place, and may have been in the same spot. I remember specifically one image an event that occurred in the renascence era at or near this same old tree. Whether the tree was alive or not, it definitely held these secrets, and I certainly believe their truth.

I had also come to realize very young that I had another ability ("talent") dealing with ghosts. At first I never understood the strong and sometimes-scary feeling I would get in places where someone may have died or where a spirit was living, visiting, or stuck. It took for me to have those feelings, keep them quiet and then hear stories of those same places, and what had happened to certain deceased individuals.

I have never been ashamed of my extra abilities I look at them as a blessing. In some cases they have even prevented people from seriously dangerous situations. For as long as I can I will always try to be a help to others, and give thanks for what I've been given.

—Becky, age 16